STREETWISE FRENCH

Speak and Understand Everyday French

Isabelle Rodrigues

Ted Neather

with illustrations by Chris Garratt

PASSPORT BOOKS

NTC/Contemporary Publishing Group

Library of Congress Cataloging-in-Publication Data

Rodrigues, Isabelle.
Streetwise French : speak and understand everyday French /
Isabelle Rodrigues and Ted Neather ; with illustrations by Chris Garratt.
p. cm.
Includes bibliographical references.
ISBN 0-658-00416-6
1. French language—Slang. 2. French language—Textbooks for foreign speakers—English. I. Neather, Ted. II. Title.
PC3739.R63 2000
448.3'421—dc21 00-37349
CIP

Cover design by Nick Panos
Cover photograph copyright © Suzanne and Nick Geary/Stone
Interior design by Precision Graphics
Interior illustrations by Chris Garratt

Published by Passport Books
A division of NTC/Contemporary Publishing Group, Inc.
4255 West Touhy Avenue, Lincolnwood (Chicago), Illinois 60712-1975 U.S.A.

Printed in the United States of America
International Standard Book Number: 0-658-00416-6
01 02 03 04 05 06 LB 15 14 13 12 11 10 9 8 7 6 5 4 3 2 1

Contents

Introduction viii

Chapitre 1:
Salut! Ça va? Comment vas-tu? 2
Greeting people • Asking how they are • Saying how you feel

Language and culture: *Forms of address—using **tu** and **vous** • **Monsieur/Madame** • Greeting people* 10

Chapitre 2:
Y a de l'abus! Y en a vraiment ras le bol! J'en ai marre! 14
Complaining about unfair treatment • Giving someone a piece of your mind

Chapitre 3:
Excusez-moi Monsieur. Vous ne sauriez pas où est . . . ? 28
Asking the way • Understanding directions

Language and culture: *Pronunciation* • *Grammatical patterns* 37

Chapitre 4:
T'as pas 100 balles à me filer? Ça serait chouette! 40
Asking a favor • Convincing/persuading someone to do something

Chapitres de révision 1–4: Review of Chapters 1–4 52

Chapitre 5:
Ça n'a pas l'air de tourner rond. Trouve une combine! T'en fais pas. 56
Giving someone moral support • Giving advice

Language and culture: ***Argot, verlan,** and **la langue des banlieues*** 67

CHAPITRE 6:
ALORS, ÇA S'EST BIEN PASSÉ? TU AS L'AIR FORTEMENT SECOUÉ! ÇA ME SCIE! 70
Telling a story • Expressing surprise

CHAPITRE 7:
ENTRE NOUS DEUX, C'EST COOL. J'SUIS RAIDE DINGUE DE TOI. IL EST FRANCHEMENT CRAQUANT! 82
Expressing your feelings • Using expressions of love and affection

Language and culture: *Love, sex, and togetherness* 93

CHAPITRE 8:
C'EST TOUJOURS HYPER-BONDÉ; GRAND COMME UN MOUCHOIR DE POCHE; UNE MEUF AGUICHANTE ET MARRANTE 96
Describing places • Describing people

CHAPITRE 9:
J'AVAIS CRAQUÉ POUR LUI. ÇA NE COLLAIT PAS. JE L'AI PLAQUÉ. 110
Talking about the past • Remembering

Language and culture: *Changing society, changing language* 121

CHAPITRES DE RÉVISION 5–9: REVIEW OF CHAPTERS 5–9 125

CHAPITRE 10:
ÇA TE BRANCHERAIT PAS? ÇA ME SEMBLE UN BON PLAN. ON POURRAIT PRENDRE MA CAISSE. 130
Making plans • Explaining your intentions

CHAPITRE 11:
ÇA TE DONNE UN LOOK PLUS COOL. TU ES DRÔLEMENT BIEN SAPÉ! 144
How to pay compliments and how to accept them • Gossiping

Chapitre 12:
On a une grosse galère. C'est râpé. On aurait eu du fun! 158
Telling someone how disappointed/how enthusiastic you are

Language and culture: *The varieties of French and* ***la francophonie*** 170

Chapitre 13:
C'est de la daube! J'en avais ma claque!
C'est franchement délire! 172
Saying what you like and don't like • Expressing your views and your preferences • Saying that you agree or disagree

Chapitre 14:
Ça s'arrose à mort! À la tienne! À la nôtre! 184
Ordering in a restaurant • Proposing a toast

Language and culture: *Eating and drinking* 195

Chapitres de révision 10–14: Review of Chapters 10–14 198

Answers to Exercises 202

French-English Glossary 209

Select Bibliography 229

Introduction

Anyone, however well they know a foreign language, can run into problems of comprehension in certain circumstances. Often, this is because courses in a foreign language do not prepare you for colloquial language, or perhaps even slang, which is part of the everyday speech of many native speakers. And when you start to get the hang of colloquial language, you may run into another problem. Perhaps you can understand it, but how much of this language can you personally use?

It is important, when you learn a foreign language, to be aware of what linguists call "register." What level of language, formal or informal, neutral or vulgar, is appropriate to use in any particular situation? To answer this question, let's start by dividing colloquial language into three main levels.

First, there are the words and expressions that form part of the everyday language of most people in relaxed situations. For example, you might not refer to "a man" but to "a guy." In the same way, in French, you might talk about "un mec." You would hope to understand this sort of language and to use it yourself in the right contexts.

Next, there is the racier slang, which would be used by young people among themselves, or which might be particular to a group sharing a common interest. Again, you might want to understand this sort of slang, but it is doubtful whether you would want to use it yourself, unless you were the same age or part of the same "group" as the others.

Finally, there is the point at which colloquial language becomes not just popular but vulgar. This is what the French call **langue verte.** Here, you need to be very careful, when using the foreign language, not to offend or shock your listeners. But it can be amusing to understand this **langue verte,** whether in real life, or, perhaps, in a movie.

So in this book we have set for ourselves the following important objectives:

- to provide a variety of authentic situations with participants of different ages and circumstances, talking quite naturally
- to offer comprehension exercises, which allow you to understand and learn a range of colloquial or slang expressions

It is difficult to be precise when allocating words to a particular register. Language is changing all the time; expressions that were definitely to be avoided only a few years ago are now part of colloquial language. So we have given full explanations in the language notes to each chapter and marked with an **asterisk** expressions that are probably not for you to use personally, unless you know your companions well; even then, you may get it wrong!

The layout of the book is as follows:

Chapters and dialogues. The fourteen chapters each focus on certain functions in language, as indicated in the chapter headings. Each chapter contains two dialogues where French people, mainly of a younger age-group, use a variety of colloquial language for expressing these functions. One dialogue gives an example of Canadian French (**québécois**), but the others concentrate on French as spoken in France.

English translations of the dialogues. Translations that are specifically British English appear in parentheses.

Vocabulary notes after each dialogue, in a section titled **Attention au langage familier!** This section gives literal translations of the idioms, where this is helpful, and provides detailed notes about usage.

A variety of exercises, in a section titled **À votre tour!** to check your understanding of the dialogues and your ability to use the idioms yourself.

Vocabulary lists to assist with the exercises, covering the whole chapter, including dialogues, jokes, and cultural sections.

Authentic jokes in some of the chapters, entitled **Histoires drôles,** follow the theme of the chapter and make use of word plays and puns, which help the understanding of the language.

Language and culture. In seven of the chapters there is a short essay on a linguistic/cultural theme. These explain some of the background to recent developments in the colloquial language and link these developments to social trends and the French language's place in the wider world (**la francophonie**).

Review chapters provided at three points in the book, entitled **Chapitres de révision,** each with a crossword puzzle and exercises, review the previous four or five chapters.

The answer key at the end of the book provides answers for all exercises in the chapters and review sections.

A French-English glossary at the end of the book contains a valuable reference list, in alphabetical order, of all the words and expressions contained in the vocabulary lists of each chapter.

Original drawings by Chris Garratt give a humorous angle on the language functions and key idioms of each chapter.

It is always stimulating to make contact with the real spoken language as it adapts to changing social trends and new developments in technology. We hope that *Streetwise French* will give you a real flavor of the state of the spoken language in the new millennium, and we encourage you to try out new words and expressions when you next visit France or a French-speaking country.

STREETWISE FRENCH

. Chapitre 1 .

Salut! Ça va? Comment vas-tu?

Greeting people
•
Asking how they are
•
Saying how you feel

Conversation 1

Trois étudiants se rencontrent à la cafétéria de la fac.

Sam **Salut** Oli, **ça va?**

Oli Pas mal et toi?

Sam **Bof** . . . j'ai plutôt la **gueule de bois** ce matin! Hier soir on avait décidé de se faire **une petite bouffe** chez Stéphanie et puis vers la fin de la soirée Paul **s'est ramené** avec deux bouteilles de gin! J'te raconte pas! J'ai **pris** une de ces **cuites!**

Oli Oui, avec **la tronche** que tu **te tapes** ce matin, **on pige** tout de suite! **Pas de bol** pour moi, je voulais **des tuyaux** pour le devoir qu'on doit rendre lundi.

Sam Alors, ça non, vraiment pas aujourd'hui, **mon vieux.** Mais on pourrait en discuter demain si tu veux. J'ai **filé** un **rencard** à Emilie ici à quatre heures.

Three students meet up at the faculty bar.

SAM Hi, Oli, how's it going?

OLI Not so bad. How about you?

SAM Don't ask! I've got a hangover (a mouth like a camel's bum) this morning. Last night we decided to have a meal (a nosh-up) at Stephanie's place and then, to finish off the evening, Paul turned up with two bottles of gin. You can guess the rest! I got hammered.

OLI Well, yeah, with that wasted look on your face this morning, I know exactly (straight off) what you mean. Well, what a bummer. I just wanted you to give me a few tips for the work we've got to hand in on Monday.

SAM Oh no, give me a break! I really can't handle that today. We can talk about it tomorrow if you like. I've got a date with Emily here at four o'clock.

OLI Je **serai** pas **de trop** au moins?

SAM **Pauv' tache!** C'est aussi pour le devoir de maths qu'elle vient!

ATTENTION AU LANGAGE FAMILIER!

- **salut:** informal greeting, equivalent to "Hi."
- **Ça va?** standard way of greeting a friend and asking how he or she is. (See note in Language and Culture section of this chapter.)
- **bof!** Say it, shrugging your shoulders, to mean "Well, not so good really!"
- **la gueule de bois:** literally, "a mouth made of wood." Here it means you've got a hangover. The word **gueule** is normally only used for the mouth of an animal, so when used for a person it usually has a pejorative sense. For example, **tirer la gueule** or **faire la gueule** means "to look sulky," or "to look bad tempered," and **Il a une sale gueule** means "I don't like the look of him." Other expressions are insulting, such as **ta gueule!** ("Shut your trap!"). But in the right context, some familiar expressions are quite affectionate, for example, **Il a une gueule bien sympathique** ("He looks like a really nice guy") and **Elle a une belle gueule** ("She's a really nice-looking girl").
- **une bouffe:** a general word for food or a meal: "grub" ("nosh"). Note also the verb **bouffer** and the title of the film ***La Grande Bouffe.***
- **Il s'est ramené:** "He turned up." "He rolled up."
- **prendre une cuite:** one of the many expressions for getting drunk ("to have a skinful"); "to get plastered or hammered." Also **se payer une cuite.**
- **la tronche:** slang for "face" or "head"; "ugly face" ("mug"). It can also be used to describe someone who is not looking too well: **Il doit être fatigué—il a une sale tronche.**

OLI I won't be a third wheel (playing gooseberry), will I?

SAM Don't be an idiot (a sad git)! She's coming about the math(s) work as well.

OLI TOMBE SUR LE PÈRE DE SAM.

(See Conversation 2.)

- **se payer:** has a number of uses, for example, **se payer une cuite** means "to get plastered"; **se payer une bonne grippe** means "to get a bad dose of flu"; **se payer une sale tronche** means "to look really rough"; (also **se taper une sale tronche**). When used with **tronche** ("face") in this way, the expression needs a negative adjective, such as **sale,** but this is not necessary when you have an exclamation like, **Tu vois la tronche qu'il se paye!** This clearly means "Just take a look at him! He looks absolutely awful!"
- **on pige:** a slang verb for "to understand"; "to get the drift"; "to get it." So if you understand nothing at all, you can say, **J'y pige que dalle:** "I don't understand a single thing."
- **pas de bol: bol** is a slang word for "luck," so this means "I'm out of luck."

CONVERSATION 2

*Oli **tombe sur** le père de Sam en rentrant chez lui.*

M. LAGORCE Oli! Comment vas-tu?

OLI Bonjour Monsieur. Ça va pas trop mal. Je viens juste de passer un moment avec Sam.

M. LAGORCE J'espère qu'il travaillait au moins? Mais dis donc, ça fait **un bout de temps** que je ne t'ai pas vu. Qu'est-ce que tu deviens?

OLI **Ben,** vous savez que j'ai déménagé, Sam vous l'a pas dit? Je loue une petite **piaule** juste à la limite de Paris, dans le 11ème. Alors je viens moins de votre côté. En plus, **je suis salarié** cette année alors j'ai pas beaucoup de temps non plus.

M. LAGORCE Dis donc, tu n'arrêtes pas! **Il faut que je me sauve:** Je suis **à la bourre** là. J'ai un rendez-vous dans dix minutes. Écoute, viens donc déjeuner dimanche avec nous. On aura plus de temps pour bavarder.

OLI C'est **sympa,** merci. Alors à dimanche.

- **des tuyaux:** "a few tips."
- **mon vieux:** a friendly way of addressing an old friend.
- **un rencard:** "a date," "a meeting"; **filer un rencard** is to "make a date."
- **Je serai pas de trop?** Say this if you want to be sure that you won't be a third wheel ("playing gooseberry") by joining your friends and making a threesome. Would they rather be just two? Will you be **de trop?**
- **pauv' tache:** a bit of an insult, but acceptable between friends. **Tache** usually means "a stain" or "blot," but applied in this way to a person it means someone who is a "jerk," "idiot" ("git" or "berk")!

Oli bumps into Sam's father on his way home.

MR. LAGORCE Hello, Oli. How are you?

OLI Hello, Mr. Lagorce. I'm not too bad, thanks. I've just been chatting with (to) Sam.

MR. LAGORCE At least I hope he was working? You know, it's been some time since I saw you. What have you been up to?

OLI Well, I've moved (my digs). Didn't Sam tell you? I'm renting a little crash pad on the outskirts of Paris, in the 11th. So I don't get to visit your side of town so much. Besides, I've got a job now, so I don't have a lot of time either.

MR. LAGORCE You never stop, do you! Anyway, I've got to be going. I'm running late for an appointment in ten minutes. Look, why don't you come and have Sunday lunch with us. That'll give us more time to chat.

OLI That's cool, thanks. See you Sunday, then.

ATTENTION AU LANGAGE FAMILIER!

- **tomber sur quelqu'un:** means "to bump into somebody."
- **un bout de temps:** means "quite a while."
- **ben:** common pronunciation in everyday speech instead of **bien.**
- **une piaule:** is "a place to live," "a pad," or "a room."
- **Je suis salarié:** Many French students take on a job during their studies and are called **étudiants salariés.**
- **Il faut que je me sauve:** "I must be going." "I must be on my way."
- **Je suis à la bourre:** is a common way of saying, "I'm late."
- **sympa:** an abbreviated form of **sympathique,** meaning "nice," "cool."

VOCABULAIRE DU CHAPITRE

ben (= bien)	well
bise: faire la bise	to kiss (on both cheeks)
bof	expression meaning "not too well," "so-so"
bol: avoir du bol	to be in luck
la bouffe	the food, a meal
bourre: être à la bourre	to be late
un bout de temps	quite a while
Ça va?	How are things? How are you doing?
cuite: (prendre) une cuite	(to get) drunk
dis donc	tell me, say
filer un rencard	to make a date
la gueule de bois	hangover
Ça marche	It's OK. It's fine.
la piaule	room, pad (digs)
piger	to understand

que dalle	nothing at all (sod all)
le rencard	date
salarié	in a job, wage earning
Salut!	Hi!
se faire une bouffe	to prepare a meal
se payer une cuite	to get plastered
se ramener	to arrive unexpectedly
se sauver	to leave in a hurry
se taper une sale tronche	to look dreadful
sympa (= sympathique)	nice, cool
une tache	spot, blot, jerk, idiot (git, berk)
tomber sur quelqu'un	to bump into someone
la tronche	face
trop: être de trop	to be a third wheel (to play gooseberry)
tutoyer	to say **tu** to somebody
le tuyau	piece of advice
vieux, mon	my old pal (my old mate)
vouvoyer	to say **vous** to somebody

À VOTRE TOUR!

A. Match the expression on the left with its equivalent on the right.

1. Salut.
2. Bof.
3. Se faire une bouffe.
4. J'ai la gueule de bois.
5. Il a pris une cuite.
6. Il a une sale tronche.
7. Il m'a filé un bon tuyau.
8. J'ai une piaule dans le coin.

a. J'ai des maux de tête dus à l'excès d'alcool.
b. Ma chambre se trouve près d'ici.
c. Il n'a pas l'air en forme.
d. Il m'a donné un bon renseignement.
e. Cuisiner un repas.
f. Pas trop bien.
g. Bonjour.
h. Il s'est soûlé.

B. Complete the expressions to fit the situation.

1. You tell a good friend you had too much to drink yesterday.
   Hier soir on a bu trois bouteilles avec Oli. Ce matin j'ai ____________. Impossible de me concentrer!
2. You want to tell a friend you found a small place to live.
   Ça fait un moment que je cherche, mais je viens de trouver ____________ près de la gare St Lazare.
3. You want to point out to your friend a guy who's not looking good.
   Regarde discrètement celui qui vient d'entrer. T'as vu ____________ qu'il se paye!
4. You want to tell your friend you have a date with a girl.
   Tu sais, ça y est: j'ai parlé à Anne et je lui a donné ____________ jeudi soir après le cours de maths.
5. You tell a friend you are out of luck today.
   J'avais tout révisé sauf l'économie en Finlande. Je lis la question. ____________ c'était justement ça!

C. Choose the most correct word to finish each statement.

1. En France quand on rencontre une personne plus âgée que soi on dit:
   a. Salut
   b. Bonjour
   c. Mes hommages

2. Si on a de bons renseignements, ou si on connaît des moyens d'obtenir quelque chose, ce sont:
   a. des infos
   b. des tuyaux
   c. des rencards

3. Vous parlez à une personne plus âgée (Pierre Durand) que vous ne connaissez pas bien. Vous lui dites:
   a. Monsieur
   b. Mon vieux
   c. Pierre

LANGUAGE AND CULTURE

The language you use is closely tied to your age, your occupation, the circles you move in, and the person you are talking to. As each generation of young people grows up, they re-create and reinvent their mother tongue, and the slang of one generation is soon overtaken by the inventions of the next. In the same way, different jobs develop their own jargon. Language also expands because of new influences from outside.

This process of change has been accelerated in this century, and, in particular, in the last twenty years, by the spread of global communication systems and the growth of new technologies, for example, the Internet, which urgently need to establish their own vocabulary. In the Language and Culture sections of this book, we will be looking at some of these developments and at the interaction between cultural and linguistic change. There are a number of signposts through this complicated terrain, and in Chapitres 1 and 3 are some clear starting points for you to come to grips with "streetwise French."

The point was made in the Introduction that "register" refers to the language that is appropriate in a particular situation. A lot of jokes rely on the basic idea that people make fools of themselves when they use the wrong language at the wrong time. What is shockingly crude in some contexts may be standard usage among certain groups of friends. But there are some basic points, particularly about the way to address people, which provide a good starting point.

FORMS OF ADDRESS—USING **TU** AND **VOUS**

The rules for using the informal **tu** or the formal **vous** are easy to summarize, but may be complicated to use. People call each other **tu** (**tutoyer**), when they are close friends or lovers; when they form part of a recognizable group, for example, all students or all members of a particular profession (but this is not always clear!); when they are adults talking to children; or when they are members of the same family. (But there are some variations here; for example, it would be normal for the husband or wife to call his or her parents-in-law **vous.**) As you can see, there are already some exceptions to these rules, and there are even husbands and wives, at a certain rather snobbish level of society, who call each other **vous** (**vouvoyer**). In the dialogues of Chapitre 1, Oli and Sam are obviously good friends who call each other **tu,** but when Oli meets Sam's father, it is immediately **Bonjour Monsieur** and the use of **vous.** It is quite unimaginable that Oli could use **tu** in such a situation. However, Monsieur Lagorce is older than Oli, knows him as a friend of his son, and has possibly known him since he was quite young, so he feels perfectly at ease calling him **tu.** The first name is always used with **tu.** Whereas the formal address (**Monsieur . . .** or **Madame . . .**) is usual with **vous,** there is a sort of in-between stage where **vous** may be used with the first name.

But things can be more complicated than this! Here is the response of a senior administrator in a government office in Paris, when asked the question: **Qui tutoies-tu? Qui vouvoies-tu?**

> My superiors? Well yes, I call the big boss **vous.** And also the principal secretary of the group who is in charge of everything including the big boss.
>
> But my line manager I call **tu,** because one day I'll step into his job, and we are both members of the same group of senior executives. The same is true if we went to the same institution of higher education, whatever difference there might be in our ages. And what do they call me? Well, my immediate boss calls me **tu** in return, but the others call me **vous.** But the principal secretary of the group uses my first name, although he calls me **vous.**
>
> It gets more complicated with my subordinates! Sometimes I might call them **tu,** but it is tricky and quite unusual, because they might take it the wrong way! I call them **vous** and use their first name.
>
> In my free time I go to the gym, and I call the women, the guys the same age as me, and the younger ones **tu.** But the younger ones reply with **vous!** I do usually call younger people **tu,** but social class might then also have a role to play!

As you can see, it's not easy! With your friends, you can be sure that **tu** is all right. Otherwise, as a foreigner, use **vous** if in doubt, and wait until the person you are with suggests that you both use **tu.**

MONSIEUR/MADAME

There is no real equivalent in English for the French use of **Monsieur** and **Madame.** In English, you would very rarely, if ever, call anyone sir or madame! But in French, it's normal to use this title for addressing anybody you don't know, or when you must use a polite form of address. And besides saying **Bonjour Monsieur** or **Madame** when you meet an individual, remember that the French are still very formal (and polite) when they enter a shop or a café where there are a number of people. So when Marc and

Éloïse go into a café in Conversation 2 of Chapitre 3 they greet everyone there: **Bonsoir messieurs-dames.** You would expect them to say, **Au r'voir messieurs-dames** as they leave. There are several other polite turns of phrase in the dialogues of Chapitre 3. For example, note the use of the conditional in phrases such as, **Vous ne sauriez pas où elle est?** and **Je me demande si vous pourriez nous aider.**

GREETING PEOPLE

You've seen that a formal greeting is **Bonjour Monsieur** or **Bonjour Madame,** followed by **comment allez-vous?** When close friends meet, it is usual for a man and woman to **faire la bise.** This is the friendly kiss on each cheek. (Maybe twice on each cheek in some parts of France!) If you look at Chapitre 11, Julien meets up with Fabienne, and says, **Fabienne! Salut! On se fait la bise.** The Americans and English have gotten used to kissing more than they used to, so perhaps this is no longer an unusual cultural habit. With Julien, as with Sam, in Chapitre 1, **salut** is the standard greeting among friends.

. Chapitre 2 .

Y a de l'abus! Y en a vraiment ras le bol! J'en ai marre!

Complaining about unfair treatment • Giving someone a piece of your mind

Conversation 1

Albert et Richard vont déjeuner dans un petit resto. Après vingt minutes ils ne sont toujours pas servis. Albert appelle le garçon.

Albert — Ça fait déjà vingt minutes qu'**on poireaute.** Écoutez, **y a de l'abus.** Je vous avais dit qu'on était **à la bourre.** C'est **se ficher du monde!**

Le Garçon — Ça vient, ça vient. (*tout bas*) **Y a pas l'feu,** non!

Dix minutes plus tard

Richard — Écoute, je commence à **saturer grave.** Y en a vraiment **ras le bol . . . On se casse?**

Le Garçon — Voilà, voilà . . . Un hamburger frites et une omelette aux champignons.

Y A VRAIMENT DE L'ABUS.

Albert and Richard go for a meal in a little restaurant. Twenty minutes later they still haven't been served. Albert calls over the waiter.

ALBERT We've been hanging around (dossing about) waiting for twenty minutes already. It's really too much to put up with! I told you that we were pressed (pushed) for time. This is really pushing it. (Is this a wind-up?)

WAITER It's on its way. (*quietly*) What's the rush? (Where's the fire?)

Ten minutes later

RICHARD Really, we've had it up to here. Shall we beat it?

WAITER OK, here it is. One hamburger and fries (chips) and one mushroom omelette.

RICHARD Pardon. **C'est quoi ça?** Vous appelez ça un hamburger, vous? Mais il est complètement **cramé!** C'est une **blague** ou quoi? Et vous croyez que je vais **bouffer** ça?

ALBERT Écoutez, on peut voir le patron?

M. PIERRE Messieurs, je suis vraiment désolé. Le chef est absent et son remplaçant est un peu **débordé.** Quand **on démarre, ça cafouille** un peu au début! Je vous apporte **des rillettes:** vous m'en **direz des nouvelles. Aux frais de la maison** bien sûr. **Ça marche?** Et excusez-moi.

ATTENTION AU LANGAGE FAMILIER!

- **poireauter:** means "to hang around waiting and getting very impatient." You might also hear **faire le poireau.**
- **Y a de l'abus:** "They are pushing their luck!" "They are going too far!"
- **à la bourre:** "running late" ("pushed for time") (see note on page 8)
- **se ficher du monde** and **se foutre du monde:** The verbs **ficher** and **foutre** in a variety of expressions are essential to understanding streetwise French. Either can be used in the expressions given here, but **ficher** is much more mild than **foutre** and is used less nowadays. So, all the examples here will show the use of **foutre.** At the most basic level, **foutre** is just a colorful variation on **faire,** so you will hear statements like, **Mais qu'est-ce qu'ils foutent** (Conversation 2 of this chapter), and questions such as, **Qu'est-ce qu'il vient foutre ici?** There are a number of fixed expressions using **foutre,** which are all rather forceful and certainly not polite, for example, **Fous-moi la paix★** ("Leave me alone"); **Fous le camp★** ("Beat it!" "Push off!"); **foutre en l'air★** ("to ruin completely," for example, **le mauvais temps a foutu nos plans en l'air**). The expression **foutre à la porte★** means "to throw out," and **se foutre de** means "to make fun of someone," ("to take the mickey," "to take the piss") as in **se foutre du monde★.** A common version of "I don't give a damn" is **Je m'en fous★** (more politely, **Je m'en fiche**), and the

RICHARD What is this? Call that a burger? It's been burned to a crisp (cinder). Are you joking (having a laugh) or what? You think I can eat that?

ALBERT Hang on. Let's have a word with the boss.

MR. PIERRE I'm very sorry. Our chef is away and his stand-in is a bit overwhelmed. When you start off, it's always a bit crazy (a bit of a cock-up). I'll bring you two meat sandwiches. You must tell me what you think of them—on the house, of course. Are you happy with that? My apologies.

---

past participle **foutu*** means that something is "completely ruined," "finished." One of the meanings of **foutre** is "to fuck," which is why a particularly crude insult is, **va te faire foutre*.**

- **Y a pas l'feu:** literally "There isn't a fire," meaning "What's the rush?" "Hang loose."
- **saturer:** means "to have enough," "to have it right up to here." In the conversation Richard might also say, **J'en ai marre,** and he underlines it when he says, **Y en a vraiment ras le bol,** which has the same meaning.
- **grave:** The adjective is used, very unusually, instead of the adverb one might expect after a verb. It has the effect of reinforcing the power of the verb, and used with **saturer** here, it means "I've really had just as much as I can take."
- **ras le bol:** very common expression for having as much as you can take. It can also be used as a noun, so that **le ras-le-bol** means "the absolute limit of what anyone can accept."
- **on se casse:** means "to leave in a hurry," "to beat it," "to split."
- **C'est quoi ça?** Spoken with heavy sarcasm, it means "Just what do you think that's supposed to be?"
- **cramé:** This word has been borrowed from the Occitan language of the south of France and means "burned to a crisp (cinder)."
- **blague:** "a joke."

- **bouffer:** is the most common slang word for "to eat." The noun, **la bouffe,** meaning "food" or "a meal," is found in many expressions; for example, **C'est pas l'heure de la bouffe? On va acheter de la bouffe? On se fait une petite bouffe?**
- **débordé:** "completely overwhelmed," usually by work.
- **on démarre:** This verb is usually used for motor vehicles starting up and going away. By extension, it can mean anything starting up and going on.
- **ça cafouille:** a common expression for "There's a mess" ("a balls-up"). Linked to this, **un cafouillage** is a lack of organization, and **un cafouilleur** is somebody totally disorganized who makes a mess (creates a balls-up).
- **des rillettes:** Monsieur Pierre offers them **rillettes,** as this is a particular delicacy, a sort of canned meat.
- **dire des nouvelles:** The basic meaning of **une nouvelle** is "a piece of news," as in **une bonne nouvelle; une mauvaise nouvelle.** It can also be used in the plural, for example, **Vous avez de ses nouvelles?** "Have you heard from him/her?" If you ask someone to try out a new drink or a new dish, you can say **Vous m'en direz des nouvelles** and it means "I'm sure you'll like it," which is the way it is used here. There is another, rather similar expression, when someone has let you down or messed with you, and you say, **Il aura de mes nouvelles** "I'll give him a piece of my mind!"

CONVERSATION 2

Marc et Anne font la queue au guichet pour acheter des billets pour un concert.

ANNE Ça n'avance pas **d'un poil.** A force de **se faire rincer,** on va être **trempé jusqu'aux os.**

MARC Mais **qu'est-ce qu'ils foutent! J'en ai** vraiment **marre de poireauter** ici. Tu vas voir on va **se choper** une bronchite **par-dessus le marché!** J'vais aller les **remuer** un peu, moi, attends!

- **aux frais de la maison:** Used by itself, the expression **au frais de** means "at the expense of." You might say **à mes frais** if you were saying, "it's on me." Here, **la maison** refers to the restaurant, so he is saying, "It's on the house."
- **Ça marche?** "Is that OK?" "Does that suit you?" This is a variation on **Ça va?** with the same sort of meaning.

Marc and Anne are waiting in line (queuing) at the ticket office to buy tickets for a concert.

ANNE We haven't moved an inch. And with it pouring rain (chucking it down), we'll get soaked to the bone (skin).

MARC What are they doing (playing at)! I'm absolutely sick of hanging around (about) here. And we're going to get pneumonia on top of it all. Just you wait. I'm going to stir them up a bit.

Marc tape au carreau pour attirer l'attention de l'employé.

MARC Dites donc, vous savez qu'il y a des gens qui **poireautent.** C'est un comble ça alors! Pendant qu'**on se les gèle** ici, vous **papotez** au téléphone. C'est **dingue! Faut pas pousser** quand-même. Vous pourriez choisir un autre moment, non?

*L'employé raccroche, l'air **furax.** Le téléphone sonne de nouveau. Il décroche encore.*

ANNE J'y crois pas, **il remet ça.** Il en a vraiment **rien à secouer** de ce que tu viens de lui dire.

MARC Ce coup-ci je sens que je vais **péter un plomb.**

ATTENTION AU LANGAGE FAMILIER!

- **pas d'un poil:** The word **poil** actually means "hair," but this expression means a "very small amount."
- **se faire rincer:** They are standing in the rain and getting absolutely soaked.
- **trempé jusqu'aux os:** Literally "soaked to the bones."
- **J'en ai marre.** This is the most common expression for saying, "I've had enough already." "I've had just as much as I can take." See also **J'en ai ras le bol** (Chapitre 9, page 113) and **J'en ai ma claque** (Chapitre 13, page 175).
- **se choper:** The verb **choper** means "to catch," "to seize." To get caught by the police would be **se faire choper par les flics.** So here, the idea is that they might catch a cold.
- **par-dessus le marché:** "to top it all" ("to crown it all").
- **remuer:** usually means "to stir" but here has the sense of "to get them moving."
- **On se les gèle:** means "We're getting really cold," but it is a shortened version of **On se gèle les couilles,** meaning "Our balls are freezing." It sounds like the French version of "brass monkeys"!

Marc taps on the window to attract the attention of the salesperson.

MARC Hey! Did you know there are people waiting here? It's a disgrace. We're frozen stiff while you're chatting (gassing) on the phone. It's mad. You're really pushing it. Can't you call some other time?

The salesperson hangs up looking steamed. The telephone rings and he picks it up again.

ANNE (to Marc) I don't believe it! He's at it again. He doesn't give a damn (a toss) about what you've just told him.

MARC You're right. This time I'm really going to blow a fuse!

- **papoter:** a colloquial word for "to chatter" ("to have a natter").
- **dingue:** is a very common word for "mad," "crazy."
- **Faut pas pousser:** means "Don't push your luck!"
- **furax:** is a popular variation of **furieux,** meaning "really mad."
- **Il remet ça:** "He's starting again." "He's at it again." "He doesn't know when to stop."
- **Il en a rien à secouer:** "He's taking absolutely no notice." "He doesn't give a damn (a toss)."
- **péter un plomb:** The verb **péter** is commonly used for "to break," "to blow up," "to break down." (It can also mean "to fart.") So you will hear **Il s'est pété sur l'autoroute,** and **La lampe ne marche plus, l'ampoule est pétée.** Here the meaning is "to blow a fuse" ("to bust a gut").

VOCABULAIRE DU CHAPITRE

abus: Y a de l'abus!	That's going too far!
la blague	joke
bouffer	to eat

à la bourre	running late
C'est quoi ça?	What's this?
Ça marche?	Is that all right? Is that acceptable?
cafouiller	to mess things up (to make a balls of something)
choper	to catch
le comble	the absolute limit
cramer	to go up in smoke, to burn
débordé, être	to be overwhelmed (usually by work)
démarrer	to start work, to get going (starting a car)
dingue	crazy, mad
dire des nouvelles	(see note on page 18)
foutre*; Qu'est-ce qu'il fout*? en avoir rien à foutre*	to do (see note on page 16)
aux frais de	at the expense of . . .; . . . is paying
furax	really mad
grave	really (when used as an adverb)
un imper(méable)	raincoat
marché: par dessus l'marché	to top it all (crown it all)
marre: en avoir marre	to be sick of something, to have as much as you can take
papoter	to chatter
péter un plomb	to blow a fuse (to bust a gut)
péter	to blow up, to fart, to break down
pleuvoir (des cordes)	to pour with rain
un poil	a tiny bit (literally "a hair")
le poireau, faire	to hang around (about)
poireauter	to be kept waiting, to hang around
pousser: Faut pas pousser.	Don't push your luck.
râler	to moan, complain
ras le bol: en avoir ras le bol	to be sick and tired of something, to be fed up with

remettre ça	start all over again
remuer	to stir, to get someone moving
les rillettes	canned meat (made from pork or goose)
rincer, se faire	to get soaked
le salaud	bastard
le saligaud*	bastard
le salopard*	bastard
saturer	to have had enough of something
se casser*	to split, to beat it (synonym **on se tire**)
se ficher du monde	not to give (care) a damn about something
se les geler*	cold enough to freeze your balls off
secouer: n'avoir rien à secouer	(see note on page 21)
trempé (jusqu'aux os)	soaked (to the bone/skin)
Y a pas l'feu!	No rush! Calm down!

À VOTRE TOUR!

A. Choose the response that best gives the real meaning of the following idioms.

1. On est vraiment **à la bourre!**
    a. On est très pressés.
    b. On manque d'argent.
    c. On a vraiment trop mangé.

2. J'en ai **ras le bol.**
    a. Je déteste ça.
    b. Je ne supporte pas ça.
    c. J'en ai assez.

3. En ce moment, il est **débordé.**
    a. Il a beaucoup de travail.
    b. Il a un travail très difficile.
    c. Il a vraiment trop de travail.

4. J'ai **cafouillé** un moment avant de comprendre.
    a. Au début, j'ai fait de grosses erreurs.
    b. D'abord, j'ai agi d'une manière un peu désordonnée.
    c. Au commencement, je râtais tout ce que je faisais.

B. Replace the underlined expressions with their familiar/slang equivalent from the list below:

bouffer	**se casser**	**se faire rincer**	**se les geler**
le comble	**pousser**	**s'en foutre**	

1. Ils se sont faits mouiller en attendant sous la pluie. ______________________
2. J'en ai assez, je m'en vais. ______________________
3. Il ne veut pas manger à la cantine. ______________________
4. On a vraiment froid quand on attend dehors. ______________________
5. Il ne faut pas exagérer! ______________________
6. Il se moque complètement de ce qu'on vient de dire. ______________________
7. Ça alors, c'est le maximum! ______________________

C. What could you say in each situation using expressions from the chapter?

1. Say you have been waiting for twenty minutes.

    ____

2. Tell the waiter, "I told you we were in a rush."

    ____

3. Tell him it's too much.

    ____

4. Ask him what that is on your plate.

____

5. Tell him your steak is completely burned.

____

6. Tell him he is really pushing it.

____

7. Ask him if he realized people were waiting.

____

D. Complete the expressions on the left. Then match them to the English equivalent on the right.

1. Il y a la queue ici. Je ________ depuis dix minutes.
2. Vous appelez ça un steak? Mais c'est une ________?
3. Je vous remplace ce steak, ça ________?
4. J'arrive, j'arrive! ________!
5. Elle n'arrête pas de ________ au téléphone.
6. Elle en a ________ de ce que je dis.
7. J'en ai assez! je vais ________.
8. Encore au téléphone? C'est ________!

a. Crazy
b. There is no rush!
c. To blow my top
d. Doesn't give a damn (toss)
e. Is that acceptable?
f. Is this a joke?
g. I've been waiting.
h. To chat

HISTOIRES DRÔLES

Le médecin examine une femme très malade. Il se tourne vers son mari et lui demande: «Il y a longtemps qu'elle **râle** comme ça?»

«Oh oui! depuis qu'on est mariés.»

The doctor examines a very sick woman. He turns to her husband and asks him: "Has your wife been moaning like this for a long time?"

"Oh yes, ever since we were married."

(The play on words here is with the verb **râler,** which means both "to moan and groan" and "to complain," "to nag.")

★★★★★

Une secrétaire prévient le directeur de banque. «Vous avez rendez-vous avec un gros client. Surtout faites attention à bien prononcer son nom, car il est susceptible. Il s'appelle Monsieur **Chalopard.** Cha-lo-pard. D'accord?»

Le directeur se répète le nom plusieurs fois pour ne pas faire de gaffe. Quand la porte de son bureau s'ouvre il se précipite sur le client la main tendue et en lui serrant la main énergiquement lui dit «Enchanté de faire votre connaissance Monsieur **Chaligaud.**»

A secretary warns the bank manager. "You've got an appointment with an important customer. Please be especially sure to pronounce his name properly, because he's very sensitive. His name is *Chalopard,* OK?"

The manager repeats the name several times so as not to put his foot in his mouth (in it). When the office door opens, he rushes to meet the customer with his hand stretched out. He shakes the customer's hand very warmly, and says, "I'm delighted to meet you, Mr. *Chaligaud.*"

(Not translatable. The joke lies in the bank manager's trying so hard to avoid **Chalopard,** which is close to **salopard** [a variation of **salaud**], meaning "bastard," that he uses **Chaligaud,** which is close to **saligaud,** another variation of **salaud.**)

. Chapitre 3 .

Excusez-moi Monsieur. Vous ne sauriez pas où est . . . ?

Asking the way

•

Understanding directions

Conversation 1

Marc et Éloïse viennent juste d'arriver à Caen. Ils ne connaissent pas la ville et veulent trouver l'auberge de jeunesse.

Éloïse — **Merde, alors.** L'Office de tourisme vient de fermer! C'est bien notre **bol!** Comment on va la trouver cette auberge? Et on a même **paumé** le plan de la ville.

Marc — **T'inquiète! J'assure un max.** Je vais aller demander au **type** là-bas. **Il a l'air d'être du coin.** Excusez-moi Monsieur. On cherche l'auberge de jeunesse. Vous ne sauriez pas où elle est, s'il vous plaît?

Le Monsieur — Désolé, mais je **suis** juste **de passage** ici; alors je ne peux vraiment pas vous renseigner. Mais prenez la première, là, à votre gauche, il y a un petit **troquet** qui est encore ouvert. J'en sors juste. Ils sont très **sympas.** Ils vous renseigneront sûrement.

Marc and Éloïse have just arrived in Caen. They don't know the town, and they want to find the youth hostel.

ÉLOÏSE Oh shit! The tourist office has just closed. That's just our luck. How are we going to find the hostel? We haven't even got a town map (plan).

MARC Chill out! I know what we'll do. I'll just go and ask the guy over there. He looks like a local. Excuse me. We're looking for the youth hostel. Do you happen to know where it is?

PASSERBY Sorry, but I'm just passing through. I can't help you, I'm afraid. But if you take the first turn on the left there, you'll see a little café, which is still open. I've just come out of there and they are really nice (sound). They'll be sure to help you.

MARC	Merci quand même. Au revoir et bonne soirée.
LE MONSIEUR	Au revoir. Bonne chance!

ATTENTION AU LANGAGE FAMILIER!

- **Merde:** a very common swearword, not always to be translated literally as "shit" (which is stronger in British English). Depending on how and when it is said, it can be more or less insulting. A lawyer reported the story of a woman who wanted to start legal proceedings against somebody **«Qui m'avait dit merde impoliment!»** When swearing at oneself when you've done something silly, like dropping, losing, or forgetting something, **merde** is not very vulgar. (See the example in the dialogue.) But when used for telling somebody to stop talking because you find him/her boring, it is very vulgar. There is an example in a well-known comic sketch by Jean Yanne, called "the driving license." A candidate for the driving test is thuggish and threatening, and terrifies the inspector. So his reply is very direct when the inspector asks him: **«Qu'est-ce que vous répondez si je vous demande . . .» «Merde, je réponds, merde».**

- **le bol:** This is a popular way of saying "luck." Nowadays it often replaces the earlier slang form **pot.** It is used in informal contexts; otherwise, you should use the expression **pas de chance.**

- **paumer:** This is a colloquial verb to use instead of **perdre** "to lose." The past participle **paumé** has a different meaning. You apply it to someone who is "spaced out" or "completely lost" ("all at sea"). **Il est complètement paumé** means "He doesn't even know what day it is."

- **T'inquiète!** This is often used as a short way of saying, **Ne t'inquiète pas.** It's unusual to drop **pas** in negative statements. This is the only negative expression in which both **ne** and **pas** are dropped. Usually, just the **ne** is dropped, as in, **T'en fais pas; t'embête pas.**

MARC Thanks all the same. Bye. (Cheers.) Have a good evening.

PASSERBY Bye. (Cheers.) Good luck.

- **J'assure un max:** Here, the word **assurer** is given a new meaning. Until recently it just meant "to insure," for example, **Je m'assure contre le vol.** The word now has, in addition, the sense of "being in control of the situation," of "knowing exactly what's got to be done." In this phrase, **un max** is short for **au maximum.**
- **type:** This refers to a male individual. Although the term is widely used, it retains a rather abusive tone if addressed directly to someone; for example, **Vous, le grand type là-bas, venez ici.** It is quite acceptable if used to refer to someone who is not present and whom one doesn't know very well; for example, **C'est pas un grand type maigre?** Usually it has a pejorative sense when applied to someone one knows, and qualified with an adjective, such as, **sale type** or **pauvre type.** There is the same shade of meaning in an expression such as **brave type.** The idea is that this is someone pleasant but a bit of a goody-goody (nice but a bit solid). Maybe this meaning dates from a Jacques Brel song with the words, **Brave, brave, mais con à la fois.**
- **Il a l'air d'être du coin:** "He looks as if he's from the neighborhood (from hereabouts)."
- **Je suis . . . de passage:** "I'm just passing through" or "I'm a stranger here."
- **troquet:** slang word for "a little café."
- **sympa:** short for **sympathique.** Used to describe people who are pleasant, welcoming, open, and affectionate. It can also be applied to things as well as people; for example, **un petit café sympa, une boîte sympa, une bouffe sympa.**

CONVERSATION 2

Marc et Éloïse entrent dans le café.

MARC ET ÉLOÏSE **Bonsoir messieurs-dames.**

ÉLOÏSE (*Au cafetier*) Excusez-moi, Monsieur. **Je me demande si vous pourriez** nous aider. Nous cherchons l'auberge de jeunesse. Est-ce que vous sauriez où elle se trouve?

LE CAFETIER Ah, l'auberge de jeunesse . . . voyons, voyons. . . . C'est bête, mais **ça ne me revient pas.** Faut dire que **c'est plus de mon âge** . . . Attendez . . . Marcel! **Amène-toi.** On a besoin de **tes lumières!** L'auberge de jeunesse, comment on y va d'ici?

MARCEL L'auberge de jeunesse? Et bien, **c'est pas la porte à côté,** mais vous avez un bus qui vous y mène presque directement. En sortant, tournez à gauche. Vous verrez un arrêt d'autobus. Prenez le bus H et descendez à l'arrêt **CHU.** Là, vous verrez, c'est juste en face du CHU.

ÉLOÏSE Ça n'a pas l'air d'être trop **balèse.** Merci beaucoup, monsieur.

ATTENTION AU LANGAGE FAMILIER!

Depending on the situation, many of these expressions are very polite.

- **Bonsoir messieurs-dames:** is an expression used to greet a number of people. It is essential to use it when entering a café or a small shop, for example, and don't forget **au r'voir messieurs-dames** as you leave.
- **Je me demande si vous pourriez:** French tends to use rather extended phrases to be sure of being polite.
- **ça ne me revient pas:** literally means "This bit of information doesn't return to my memory." The expression is often used to

---

Marc and Éloïse go into the café.

MARC AND ÉLOÏSE Evening, everybody.

ÉLOÏSE (*to the barman*) Excuse me. I wonder if you can help us? We're looking for the youth hostel. Do you happen to know where we can find it?

BARMAN Well now, the youth hostel . . . let me see. It's silly, but it's not coming back to me. That's to say I'm getting on in years (I'm a bit past it). Wait a minute. Marcel, get your butt over here. We need to pick your brain. How do you get to the youth hostel from here?

MARCEL The youth hostel? Well it's not exactly next door, but there's a bus that will take you practically right there. As you go out of here, turn left, and you'll see a bus stop. Take the H bus and get off at the hospital. You'll see the hostel right opposite the hospital.

ÉLOÏSE That doesn't seem too difficult. Thanks a lot.

explain that you have temporarily forgotten something. Note that the sense is completely different from **il/elle ne me revient pas,** when talking of a person. The sense then is to express rejection, and that there is something about the person that you really don't like.

- **C'est plus de mon âge:** means "I'm too old for that."
- **amène-toi:** a very colloquial, and not very polite, way of saying, "Come here." It should only be used with people you know very well and in a completely informal context.
- **les lumières:** "ideas"; the expression **On a besoin de tes lumières** means "We need you to advise us." "We need you to give us ideas about something."
- **C'est pas la porte à côté:** "It's not next door."
- **le CHU: Centre Hospitalier Urbain:** CHU is an acronym meaning "hospital." There are many such acronyms in French, some of which are part of day-to-day language, such as SNCF, BAP, BTS. (See the Language and Culture section in Chapitre 9.)
- **balèse:** this word can be used to mean "brawny," describing a hefty male. By extension, it has acquired the meaning of "difficult."

VOCABULAIRE DU CHAPITRE

Amène-toi!	Come here!
assurer	to know exactly what has to be done
balèse, être	(to be) difficult (also spelled **balèze**)
bol: pas de bol	(no) luck
Bonsoir messieurs-dames.	Evening, everybody.
C'est pas de mon âge.	I'm too old for that.
C'est pas la porte à côté.	It's not next door.
Ça ne me revient pas.	I can't remember.
le CHU (= Centre Hospitalier Urbain)	hospital

coin: être du coin	to come from, to live in the area
demande: Je me demande si vous pourriez . . .	I wonder if you could possibly . . .
les lumières	ideas (**On a besoin de tes lumières,** "We need to pick your brain.")
maximum, un max	the most, absolutely
merde alors!	Shit! Damn! (Bugger!)
passage: être de passage	to be passing through
paumer quelque chose	to lose something
sympa (= sympathique)	nice, sound
T'embête pas.	Don't get worked up about it.
T'inquiète.	short for **Ne t'inquiète pas,** Don't worry.
le troquet	café, joint
le type	guy (bloke)

À VOTRE TOUR!

A. For each of the following underlined sentences, choose the sentence that has the same meaning.

1. Ce type a l'air d'être du coin.
   a. Cet homme semble habiter par ici.
   b. Il habite au coin de la rue.

2. J'assure.
   a. Je te promets de trouver une solution.
   b. Je m'y connais, tu peux me faire confiance.

3. Je suis de passage.
   a. Je viens de passer sans faire attention.
   b. Je suis ici pour peu de temps.

4. On a besoin de tes lumières.
   a. On n'y voit rien, donne-nous une lampe.
   b. Ce que tu sais va sûrement nous aider.

5. Ça ne me revient pas.
   a. J'arrive pas à m'en souvenir.
   b. Je ne peux pas vous le dire.

B. Choose the polite term from the following list on the right that best corresponds to the slang/familiar term on the left.

1. Merde.	a. J'ai la situation bien en main.
2. T'inquiète.	b. Ils sont bien aimables.
3. Ce type.	c. Quel dommage.
4. Un troquet.	d. J'aimerais que tu me renseignes.
5. Amène-toi.	e. Ne te fais pas de soucis.
6. Le bol.	f. Un café.
7. J'assure un max.	g. Un monsieur.
8. Ils sont sympas.	h. La chance.
9. On a besoin de tes lumières.	i. Viens ici.

C. Imagine the following conversation between two older people and replace the underlined familiar/slang expression by a more correct one.

M. COTREL	Je crois qu'on s'est paumé.
MME COTREL	T'inquiète! Demande à ce type là-bas. Il a l'air sympa.
M. COTREL	Vous savez où est la gare?
PASSANT	Manque de bol, j'suis pas du coin. Mais j'ai un plan, je vais vous montrer. Voilà, c'est là.
M. COTREL	Super! ça n'a pas l'air trop balèse.
MME COTREL	Alors, salut!

D. Directions.

1. Ask a passerby where the tourist office is.

____

2. Say that, unfortunately, you cannot be of any help.

____

3. Say you are just passing through.

____

4. Say you cannot remember.

____

5. Say it is not very near.

____

6. Tell her that the café has just closed.

____

7. Tell him to turn left, take bus H, and stop at the CHU.

____

8. Say it does not seem too difficult to find.

____

LANGUAGE AND CULTURE

Spoken language has its own rules of use, which vary in a number of ways from the rules you'll find in the books that try to teach "correct" French. Where pronunciation is concerned, spoken French quite commonly drops certain letters or words, and the grammar of spoken French follows its own patterns, which are usually considered ungrammatical or incorrect in the written language. Here are some basic guidelines.

PRONUNCIATION

The most common feature of the spoken language is "elision," that is, running words together and dropping unstressed letters.

The most frequently dropped letter is unstressed **e,** as in **je, te, le.** If you add to this the fact that the **ne** is almost always dropped from the negative **ne . . . pas,** you will understand common spoken forms like **j'sais pas (je ne sais pas),** which sounds like "shépa."

In the same way, **u** is dropped from **tu,** so that **tu as vu** becomes **t'as vu,** and **tu n'as qu'à** becomes **t'as qu'à,** which sounds like "taka." Suddenly, a lot of the difficulties of understanding spoken French fade away! You finally realize what all these "takas" mean. "Takalfer" is really **tu n'as qu'à le faire!** Here are some of the most common contracted forms you will hear (and, of course, soon learn to use!):

tu as: t'as

tu n'as pas: t'as pas

je suis: j'suis (sounds like *shui*)

je ne sais pas: j'sais pas (sounds like *shépa*)

je ne crois pas: j'crois pas (sounds like *shcrwapa*)

je n'y crois pas: j'y crois pas

il y a: y a (**Y a de l'abus.** Chapitre 2, Conversation 1)

il n'y a pas: y a pas

il y avait: y avait

cette: c'tte

c'était: c'té

Another little word frequently dropped is **il** in expressions using **il faut que;** for example, **Faut dire que c'est plus de mon âge** (Chapitre 3, Conversation 2).

Cela is universally shortened to **ça,** and used as an all-purpose subject or object. See, for example, Chapitre 2, Conversation 1: **ça fait vingt minutes . . . ; ça vient; Vous appelez ça un hamburger? Ça marche.**

GRAMMATICAL PATTERNS

Questions are easier to form in conversation than in the correct written language. Written French favors inversion of the verb in questions such as **Quand es-tu arrivé? Combien as-tu payé? Pourquoi avez-vous fait cela?** Spoken French has a horror of inversion and almost always uses a direct form: **T'es arrivé quand? T'as payé combien? Pourquoi vous avez fait ça? Comment on y va?** Another common way of avoiding inversion is to use the question form **est-ce que?** But even this is frequently shortened in spoken French, so that **D'où est-ce que tu viens?** becomes **D'où tu viens?** or **Tu viens d'où?** The question **qui est-ce qui?** becomes **qui c'est qui?** as in, **Qui c'est qui t'a dit ça?**

When asking the time you might hear, or say, **Quelle heure il est?** or **Il est quelle heure?** or **Quelle heure t'as?** as well as the more formally correct **Quelle heure est-il?** On the model of **Il est quelle heure?** another variation on the direct word order is to place the question word (**Quand?** or **où?** and so on) at the end of the phrase. So you get forms such as the following: **T'as payé combien? T'es arrivé quand? Tu cherches qui?** and **Ils parlent de quoi?**

Negatives have their own spoken forms. We've already seen that **ne** is universally omitted. In one expression, **t'inquiète,** both **ne** and **pas** are dropped! (See this chapter, page 30.) In giving orders in the negative, written French produces statements such as **Ne le fais pas!** or **Ne l'écoute pas!** Spoken French simplifies the construction to **Le fais pas!** or **L'écoute pas!**

Exclamations such as **Qu'elle est belle!** or **Qu'il fait chaud ici!** are expressed as **Qu'est-ce qu'elle est belle!** or **Qu'est-ce qu'il fait chaud ici!**

. CHAPITRE 4 .

T'as pas 100 balles à me filer? Ça serait chouette!

ASKING A FAVOR
•
CONVINCING/PERSUADING SOMEONE TO DO SOMETHING

CONVERSATION 1

Stéphane, vingt-deux ans, étudiant, est resté chez lui avec son jeune frère Oscar, dix-sept ans.

OSCAR Stéphane, t'as pas **100 balles à me filer?** J'ai plus une **thune.** J'peux pas aller au **ciné** avec **mes potes** ce soir. Je suis **à sec.**

STÉPHANE Encore! Tu m'as déjà **taxé 100 boules** la semaine dernière! **Abuse pas!** Cette fois, c'est non. Plus rien, mon p'tit **gars** jusqu'à ce que je revois **mon blé.**

OSCAR Charles, lui, son **frangin** c'est un vrai **pote.** Il lui a **filé** ça sans **râler.**

STÉPHANE **Tu parles!** Il est **plein aux as** son frangin. Moi, j'ai pas **un rond** en ce moment. Et puis, **fous-moi la paix.** J'ai du boulot, moi.

Stéphane, a student aged twenty-two, has stayed at home with his younger brother Oscar, who is seventeen.

OSCAR Stéphane, you couldn't slip me a ten could you? I'm broke (skint). I can't go to the movies (flicks) with my friends (mates) this evening, because I'm flat (stoney) broke.

STÉPHANE What, again! You already bummed off me (scrounged a wedge off me) only last week. Don't push your luck. This time the answer is no (you've had it). Not another penny till I see the bread, buddy (boyo)!

OSCAR Charles's bro is a real pal (mate). He handed it over without whining.

STÉPHANE So what! Well, his brother's loaded, and I haven't got a dime (bean) at the moment. Anyway, leave me alone! I've got work to do.

OSCAR Ecoute, c'est juste une avance. C'est demain que je commence à **bosser.**

STÉPHANE Mais t'es **bouché** ou quoi? J'te l'ai dit, j'ai pas **un rond.** Alors, **casse-toi . . .** et arrête de me **faire suer.** T'as qu'à aller jouer de **ta gratte** et **faire la manche** dans le métro.

OSCAR C'est malin.

ATTENTION AU LANGAGE FAMILIER!

In this dialogue are several slang words for money. **100 balles** means "100 francs." In this sense, **balles** is very common and is only used in the plural, usually for a round sum, for example, **20 balles, 50 balles**; **boules** is another possibility for **balles. Une thune** or **des thunes** is also in constant use to mean "cash," often by younger speakers in place of older slang (still widely used) such as **fric** and **pognon.** You will also hear **le blé,** which can be used in a more general sense to refer to considerable wealth, for example, **Il s'est fait beaucoup de blé dans le commerce. Des ronds** can be used to refer to money in general, but is often found, as in the dialogue above, in the negative sense, **Je n'ai plus un rond.** Although they do not occur in the dialogue here, it is worth completing this financial survey with **une brique** and **un bâton.** They are each used to mean "10,000 francs," and so can indicate large sums, for example, **un petit appart à Paris, c'est 120 briques, facile.** Someone with plenty of money is **friqué** or **plein aux as.** Finally, when you haven't got anything left, when you are completely cleaned out, you are **à sec** or **fauché**.

- **filer:** is a colloquial word for **donner.**
- **taxer:** has the sense of **emprunter,** "to borrow," but with overtones of taking for keeps, even of stealing!
- **ciné:** is short for **cinéma.** Also used as a colloquial form is **cinoche.**
- **Abuse pas!** "Don't push your luck!"
- **gars:** is a general all-purpose word for a "guy," "lad" ("bloke"). Here, **mon petit gars** is rather patronizing from the elder to the younger brother, "my lad."

OSCAR Just listen a moment. It's just a loan. Tomorrow I start working (jobbing).

STÉPHANE Are you deaf (thick) or something? I told you, I haven't got a cent (a bean), not a single dime, get it? So buzz off and stop bugging me. Why don't you just take your guitar and play for some change (go busking) in the subway (underground)?

OSCAR I suppose you think that's clever!

- **frangin:** means "brother" has a feminine form **frangine;** the two are widely used instead of **frère** and **sœur.**
- **mes potes:** "my friends," "my pals" ("my mates"). The word can be either masculine or feminine.
- **râler:** is "to complain," "to whine," "to moan," and the person who does the whining is **un râleur** (or use **râleuse**).
- **Tu parles!** "So what!"
- **Fous-moi la paix:** "Leave me alone." "Give me a break." See note on **foutre** (Chapitre 2, page 16).
- **bosser:** "to work," usually with the sense of "work hard." So **un bosseur** (or **une bosseuse**) is "a hardworking person."
- **bouché:** "stupid."
- **casse-toi:** The verb **se casser** means "Beat it." When you have to leave in a hurry, you can say **J'me casse,** but used as a command the expression **casse-toi** has much the same force as **Fous-moi la paix** or **Fous le camp.**
- **Arrête de me faire suer:** This is actually a reasonably polite way to tell someone annoying or boring to "stop giving me grief." Stéphane could have said the same thing in a more vulgar way by saying, **Arrête de me faire chier.**
- **ta gratte:** commonly used for "a guitar." It is from the expression **gratter les cordes,** "to scratch the strings."
- **faire la manche:** "to beg," "to ask for money." (Here it can mean "to busk.")

CONVERSATION 2

Oscar va voir sa grand-mère pour lui demander de lui avancer un peu d'argent.

MAMIE Oscar! Quel **bon vent** t'amène? Toi, t'es pas **dans ton assiette!** Ou il y a quelque chose qui **tourne pas rond?**

OSCAR Ben, oui, **y a de quoi!** Tous mes copains vont voir un film **génial** ce soir. Mais moi, j'peux pas y aller.

MAMIE **Je te vois venir**, toi **avec tes gros sabots!** Ça fait un moment que tu **tournes autour du pot.** Tu ferais mieux de **m'annoncer** tout de suite **la couleur,** tu crois pas? De quoi as-tu besoin?

OSCAR Ben, écoute, Mamie, si tu pouvais me **filer** 100 balles, ça serait **chouette.** Tu sais j'te les rendrai jeudi, promis, juré!

MAMIE Écoute, Oscar, **ça tombe à pic.** J'ai personne pour nourrir Félix ce week-end. Alors, **un prêté pour un rendu.** Je te donne l'argent et toi, tu viens nourrir mon chat, d'accord?

ATTENTION AU LANGAGE FAMILIER!

Of course, Oscar's grandma can't be expected to use the latest streetwise slang! Her language is colloquial without being racy!

- **Quel bon vent t'amène?** "To what do I owe the pleasure of this visit?"
- **pas dans ton assiette:** "not feeling quite yourself"; "a bit off color."
- **Quelque chose ne tourne pas rond:** "Something is not going quite right."
- **Y a de quoi:** "Something is wrong," "Something is the matter."

Oscar goes to see his grandmother to ask her for a loan.

GRANDMA Oscar, what brings you here? You don't look yourself. Or is there something the matter?

OSCAR Well, yes there is something. All my friends (mates) are going to see an awesome flick (a brill film) this evening, but I can't go.

GRANDMA Are you fishing for something? You've been beating about the bush for some time now. You'd better lay your cards on the table. How much do you need?

OSCAR Well look, Gran, if you could slip me ten bucks (ten quid), that would be great. I'll let you have it back Thursday, honest, I promise.

GRANDMA Listen, Oscar, this is very convenient (handy). There's nobody to feed Felix this weekend. So, one good turn deserves another. I'll give you the money and you can come and feed my cat. OK?

- **génial:** an all-purpose adjective for something really good. He could also have said **super.** See also **chouette,** used later in the conversation, which has the same meaning.
- **Je te vois venir . . . avec tes gros sabots:** "I can see you coming a mile off!" "I can see through you." (Literally, "I can see you coming in your great big clogs.")
- **Tu tournes autour du pot:** literally, "You're turning around the cooking pot," meaning, "You're fishing for something."
- **M'annoncer la couleur:** She tells him he should tell her what it is really about, "put his cards on the table," or, as the French says literally, "Tell me what the color really is."
- **filer:** a slang way of saying "to give," often used for money.
- **Ça tombe à pic:** "This comes at just the right moment."
- **un prêté pour un rendu:** The French means "something loaned for something given in return." It can mean "tit for tat" or "one good turn deserves another."

VOCABULAIRE DU CHAPITRE

Abuse pas!	Don't push your luck!
annoncer la couleur	to come clean, to put one's cards on the table
avoir les moyens de payer	to be able to afford it
les balles	francs
le bâton	stick, 10,000 francs
le blé	money, cash, wealth
bosser	to work
bouché	stupid
les boules	francs
le brique	brick, 10,000 francs
le caoutchouc	rubber (contraceptive)
chouette	super, great, marvelous

le ciné	cinema, pictures, movies
le cinoche	cinema, movies
le commerçant	businessman
cordes: gratter les cordes	to play the guitar
un embout de caoutchouc	a rubber tip (on the end of a walking stick)
faire chier quelqu'un	to give grief, to annoy
faire la manche	to beg, to ask for money (to busk)
faire suer	to annoy, to bore, to bug, to give grief
la famille nombreuse	large family
fauché	cleaned out (skint)
filer	to give
Fous-moi la paix!	Leave me alone! Give me a break!
foutre le camp*	to beat it (to sod off)
le frangin	brother
le fric	cash, loot, dough
friqué	loaded, wealthy
le gars	guy (bloke, lad)
génial	terrific, marvelous, brilliant, **chouette**
la gratte	guitar
le pognon	cash, loot, dough
pas dans son assiette	not feeling quite yourself, a bit off color
plein aux as	well off, loaded
le/la pote	friend, pal, mate, buddy
Un prêté pour un rendu.	tit for tat; One good turn deserves another.
Quel bon vent t'amène?	To what do I owe the pleasure of this visit?
Quelque chose ne tourne pas rond.	Something is not going quite right.
râler	to complain, to whine, to moan
rien ne se produit	nothing happens
le rond	penny, dime (sou)
sabots: Je te vois venir avec tes gros sabots.	I can see through you.

SAMU (= Service d'Assistance Médicale d'Urgence)	ambulance service
se casser	to leave, to beat it, to split
à sec	cleaned out (without a bean)
le siège	seat
super	great, first-rate, terrific
taxer	to borrow, to bum (to scrounge)
la thune	money, cash
tomber à pic	to come at just the right moment
tourner autour du pot	to fish for something
Tu parles!	So what!
y a de quoi	something is wrong, something is the matter
à zéro	rock bottom
zéro: ça me fout le moral à zéro	that makes me feel really bad

À VOTRE TOUR!

A. Match the beginning of the phrase on the left with the appropriate ending on the right.

1. Tu pourrais pas
2. J'ai même pas assez de blé
3. Bientôt j'aurai du fric
4. Si t'as tant besoin de ronds
5. Tu ferais mieux tout de suite
6. Je le vois, ça fait un moment que
7. Ça serait vraiment chouette

a. si tu pouvais me filer 100 balles.
b. de m'annoncer la couleur.
c. t'as qu'à faire la manche dans le métro.
d. tu tournes autour du pot.
e. parce que j'ai trouvé un boulot.
f. me filer 100 balles?
g. pour me payer une place de ciné.

B. Match the expressions on the left to their English equivalents on the right.

1. Fous-moi la paix!
2. Casse-toi!
3. J'te vois venir.

a. You don't look as though you are at your best.
b. I haven't got a dime (bean).

4. T'es pas dans ton assiette.	c. This comes at just the right time.
5. J'ai plus une thune.	d. One good turn deserves another.
6. Ça tombe à pic.	e. Give me a break!
7. T'es bouché?	f. Are you deaf (thick)?
8. Un prêté pour un rendu.	g. I can see through you.
	h. Beat it!

C. Choose the slang/familiar term from the following list that best corresponds to the underlined word or phrase:

un pote	**tombe à pic**	**un rond**	**me faire suer**
est plein aux as	**chouette**	**mon blé**	**frangin**
la gratte			

1. J'ai plus un sou. ____________________

2. Lui, il a énormément d'argent. ____________________

3. Ça arrive juste au bon moment. ____________________

4. Julien, c'est vraiment un ami. ____________________

5. Va jouer de la guitare! ____________________

6. Il commence à m'énerver. ____________________

7. Ce serait très gentil. ____________________

8. Son frère lui a donné du fric. ____________________

9. Quand vas-tu me rendre mon argent? ____________________

D. Write the long form of the underlined expressions.

1. Faut pas pousser.

____

2. T'as pas 100 balles?

    ____

3. J'ai pas un rond.

    ____

4. J'te l'ai pas dit?

    ____

5. T'as qu'à aller jouer de ta gratte.

    ____

6. T'es pas dans ton assiette.

    ____

7. Y a de quoi!

    ____

8. Tu crois pas?

    ____

E. Complete the expressions to fit the situation.

1. Tell him the thing to do is to play his guitar and go begging (busking) in the subway (underground).
   T'________ aller jouer de________ et ________ dans le métro.
2. Tell him that you could see through him right away.
   Je te ________, toi, avec________.
3. Ask him if he is deaf (thick).
   T'________?
4. Ask him to stop giving you grief.
   Arrête de ________.
5. Tell him that his brother is absolutely loaded.
   Son ________, il est________.

HISTOIRES DRÔLES

La femme d'un riche **commerçant** vient d'avoir un grave accident. Le médecin du **SAMU** dit à son mari, «Je vais lui faire la respiration artificielle».

«Surtout pas, Docteur. Faites-lui la vraie! **J'ai les moyens de payer.**»

The wife of a rich businessman has just had a serious accident. The doctor who comes out with the ambulance says to the husband, "I'll give her artificial respiration."

"Don't do that, doctor! Give her the real thing. I can afford it."

*****

Dans un train **une famille nombreuse** occupe tous les sièges du compartiment. Un vieil homme arrive et espère qu'un des enfants se lèvera. Mais rien ne se produit! Furax, il se met à frapper le plancher du wagon avec sa canne. Ça fait un bruit désagréable et le père de famille lui dit: «Vous devriez mettre **un embout de caoutchouc** au bout de votre canne, elle ferait moins de bruit!»

«Monsieur, si vous aviez mis **un caoutchouc** au bout de la vôtre, je serais assis, aujourd'hui!»

On the train, a family with several kids is taking up a whole compartment. An old man comes in, hoping that one of the children will get up, but nothing happens. He's really mad and starts to tap the floor of the carriage with his stick. The noise is awful, and the father says, "If you put a rubber tip on your stick it wouldn't be so noisy."

"And," says the old man, "If you'd put a rubber on yours, there would be a seat for me today."

. CHAPITRES DE RÉVISION 1–4 .

Review of Chapters 1–4

(50 points)

A. Solve the following crossword puzzle.

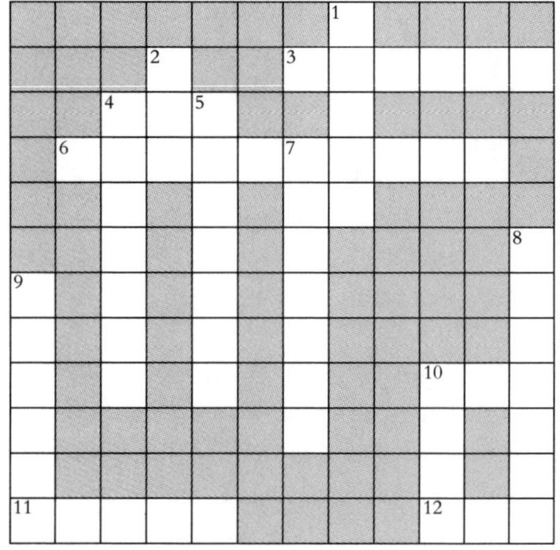

Horizontal

3. Utilisé pour dire qu'une copine n'est pas bien, pas en forme, un peu malade.
4. Trois lettres pour dire "pas formidable", "pas vraiment".
6. On nous a fait attendre.
10. Ce qui n'est pas cuit.
11. Synonyme de gentil.
12. Pronom possessif pluriel.

Vertical

1. Premier mot qu'on dit à un copain qu'on rencontre.
2. «Ce n'est pas à moi, c'est à ____.»
4. Premier mot qu'on dit à quelqu'un qu'on rencontre le matin.
5. Familier pour parler de celui qui a la même mère.
7. Etre capable de résoudre une difficulté.
8. Les chambres d'étudiants.
9. Mot à deux sens: a. désigne un jeu connu; b. avec un chiffre désigne des francs.
10. Ce qui n'est plus cru parce que cela a été transformé par l'action de la chaleur.

B. Match each French description to the correct English meaning.

15. Il m'a filé un rencard.
16. Il s'est ramené en retard.
17. Il m'a fait poireauter.

a. He is bugging me.
b. He is making fun of everyone (taking the piss).

18. Il était à la bourre.
19. Il m'a annoncé la couleur.
20. Il n'avait pas un rond.
21. Il avait paumé son porte-feuille.
22. Il m'a taxé de 100 boules.
23. Il se fiche vraiment du monde.
24. Il commence à me faire suer.

c. He bummed (scrounged) 100 francs off me.
d. He arrived late.
e. He had lost his wallet.
f. He was running late.
g. He laid his cards on the table.
h. He hadn't got a dime (bean).
i. He had given me a date.
j. He made me hang around (about) waiting.

C. Find the right word from the list to end each sentence.

gueule de bois	**bouffe**	**cuite**	**râler**
crâmer	**se casser**	**se les geler**	**péter un plomb**
avoir du bol	**pompes**	**s'éclater**	

25. Il me dit de passer chez lui. J'arrive. Il est pas là. Si je l'vois, j'te dis, je vais __________!
26. Anne n'aimait pas le quartier, elle aimait pas le resto, elle supportait pas la musique. Elle a pas arrêté de __________ toute la soirée!
27. Écoute, tu charries! Tu nous dit que tu seras là à 5h. Ça fait 20 mn qu'on __________ à t'attendre ici dehors!
28. Hier soir, pour l'anniversaire d'Antoine, j'ai exagéré je crois: on a vidé au moins trois bouteilles. Ce matin, j'ai __________.
29. Il est parti au ciné en oubliant de fermer le four! En rentrant, bonjour l'odeur! Son gratin, il était complètement __________.
30. J'veux bien faire les courses, mais j'y connais que dalle en cuisine. Il vaudrait mieux que quelqu'un d'autre se charge de la __________.
31. Les cocktails avaient l'air faciles à boire. J'en ai avalé trois sans même réaliser.
    J'ai pris une de ces __________! Je m'en souviendrai.
32. J'te préviens: je ne supporte pas les soirées guindées. Si c'est ça ce soir, j'hésite pas, je __________.
33. On est arivé 10 mn en retard, sûrs qu'on avait loupé notre train. Mais comme il avait 15 mn de retard, on l'a eu. On peut dire qu'on a eu __________.
34. Samedi soir, on est tous sortis en boîte. Y avait une ambiance super, le DJ était excellent! Qu'est-ce qu'on a pu __________!

D. The expressions underlined in the following sentences are slang and would only be used by close friends and in a very informal situation. Find from the list below the equivalent you could use safely in most situations, and rewrite the sentence using the more formal expression.

a. ennuyer	b. prêter	c. va-t'en	d. avoir froid
e. ça lui est égal	f. en avoir assez	g. rire	h. subir un échec
i. ne rien comprendre			

35. Il fait attendre tout le monde, mais ça, il n'en a rien à foutre!

____

36. T'arrives avec toutes tes histoires, quand moi je suis en plein boulot. Écoute, casse-toi!

____

37. Elle m'a fait suer toute la soirée: j'ai eu le droit à toute son histoire d'amour avec Paul.

____

38. J'ai beau lui répéter que ça ne marchera jamais entre nous, qu'il vaut mieux se quitter. Rien à faire. C'est à croire qu'elle est bouchée.

____

39. Tu pars en vacances demain? Si tu voulais bien me filer ton appart' pour une semaine, ce serait vraiment sympa.

____

40. Tu veux quand même pas qu'on reste ici à se les geler quand toi, tu es bien installé au chaud chez toi?

____

41. Tous les jours au bureau j'ai ce type sur le dos. Il arrête pas de me reprocher quelque chose. J'en ai ma claque. Je vais donner ma démission.

____

42. Henri nous a raconté toutes les histoires qui lui sont arrivées en voyage. Qu'est-ce qu'on a pu se marrer!

____

E. Choose the correct meaning for the following French words or expressions.

43. You meet a friend and ask him to come and have a drink with you. He says, «Impossible. J'ai un rencard avec Fabienne».
    a. I have a date.
    b. I have a business meeting.
    c. I have some shopping to do.

44. Someone talking about his job says, «Je commence à saturer grave».
    a. I enjoy it more and more.
    b. I really have had enough.
    c. I am very angry.

45. A friend tells you that he was so broke this summer he had to «faire la manche» in the subway (underground).
    a. to play guitar
    b. to work as a cleaner
    c. to beg

46. Fabienne tells you how impossible it is to be served in this shop because the shop's assistants «papotent» so much.
    a. are chatting with each other
    b. are complaining about work
    c. are working behind computers

47. Julien wanted to borrow money from me, but «Je l'ai vu venir avec ses gros sabots».
    a. I did not know how to refuse.
    b. I pretended I did not have any.
    c. I coud see he was fishing for something.

48. Each time I ask her to come to the movies with me, her answer is the same: «J'ai plus une thune».
    a. I do not feel well.
    b. I have too much work.
    c. I am broke (skint).

49. You drop in at a friend's house. He answers the door and says to you, «Écoute, vieux, j'suis débordé».
    a. I am up to eyes in work.
    b. I am unwell.
    c. I am on my own.

50. A friend tells you a joke and then asks you, «T'as pigé?»
    a. Did you find it funny?
    b. Did you get it?
    c. What do you think?

. Chapitre 5 .

Ça n'a pas l'air de tourner rond. Trouve une combine! T'en fais pas.

Giving someone moral support • Giving advice

Conversation 1

Amer passe chez Richard qui a pour le moment ***le moral*** *à zéro. Amer essaie de lui* ***remonter le moral.***

Amer Dis donc t'es **sourdingue** ou quoi? Ça fait trois fois que je sonne! Tu **comatais?** Je passais juste **en coup de vent** pour te dire que je fais une **teuf** chez moi vendredi soir.

Richard Pour le moment, tu sais, j'ai vraiment aucune envie de sortir.

Amer Dis-donc, toi, ça n'a pas l'air de **tourner rond.** Qu'est-ce qui t'arrive?

Richard Aurélie vient encore de **me poser un lapin.** Elle a soi-disant **chopé la crève.** Elle veut pas sortir ce soir. Faut pas **charrier,** quand-même, ça fait trois fois qu'elle me raconte les mêmes **bobards.**

Amer calls on Richard, whose morale is rock bottom at the moment. Amer tries to raise his spirits.

AMER — Hey, are you deaf or what? That's three times I've rung the bell. Were you in dreamland? I was just shooting through to tell you that I'm having a bash at my place Friday evening.

RICHARD — I don't really feel like going out, you know.

AMER — Hey, it seems like things ain't clicking (kicking). What's the problem?

RICHARD — I'm feeling down. Aurélie just stood me up again. It seems she's caught a bug. She doesn't want to go out this evening. She's pushing it. (It's a wind-up.) That's three times she's told me the same tale.

AMER Sûr, **c'est vache!** Mais c'est pas la fin du monde! C'est sûrement vrai qu'elle est **cassée.** Je l'ai vue lundi et elle avait pas l'air **dans son assiette.** Écoute, trouve une **combine** pour passer chez elle. J'sais pas, moi, achète-lui des oranges!

RICHARD Bon, tu me **boostes** un peu.

ATTENTION AU LANGAGE FAMILIER!

- **le moral à zéro:** There are a number of expressions used to describe your morale and how good you're feeling about life. If your morale is **à zéro,** you're feeling "really down," "really depressed." So it would be good to have a friend to **remonter le moral,** to "give you a lift," "raise your spirits." And if something really casts you down, say, **Ça me fout le moral à zéro.**
- **sourdingue:** means "deaf," with overtones of mockery. The normal word for "deaf" (**sourd**) has been linked with **dingue,** meaning "crazy."
- **comatais:** The verb **comater** is based on the adjective **comateux** describing somebody in a coma, or somebody who has passed out or is sleeping.
- **en coup de vent:** "in a hurry" (literally, "like a gust of wind").
- **teuf:** "party." This is the **verlan** of **fête.** (See the notes on **verlan** on pages 67–69.)
- **tourner rond:** "to be going well." **Qu'est-ce qui ne tourne pas rond?** "What's up?" "What's wrong?"
- **poser un lapin:** "to fail to turn up for a date"; "to stand someone up."
- **choper la crève:** This means "to catch a really bad cold." You can also say **attraper la crève** and **avoir la crève.** The verb **crever** means "to die" when applied to animals. It has come to

AMER Well, yeah. That sucks. (It's a pig for sure.) But it's not the end of the world. She's probably ill. I saw her Monday and she didn't look herself. Come on, think of a reason (scam) to pass by her place. I don't know. Buy her some oranges.

RICHARD OK. You've made me feel a bit better.

---

have the same meaning for people in colloquial speech; for example, **crever de faim** means "to starve to death." Of course, slang always uses forceful expressions to exaggerate and create an effect, so **Je crève de faim** is also used just to say that you are really hungry!

- **charrier:** means "to push things too far," "to exaggerate."
- **bobards:** usually found in the phrase **raconter des bobards,** "to tell fibs, lies."
- **C'est vache!** Whereas French refers to anything really bad as a "cow," in British English one is more likely to say a "pig." (American English: "That sucks.")
- **cassée:** "ill," "unwell."
- **dans son assiette:** See Chapitre 4, page 44.
- **trouver une combine:** This might also be **trouver un truc,** meaning "to find a solution to a problem," "to find a way around some difficulty."
- **booster:** "to help," "to give a lift." The word is obviously borrowed from English, and there are thousands of such words in everyday French now, such as **le parking.** Often, such borrowed words are made to fit in with the French language, so English "boost" takes on verb endings, **Tu me boostes.** Sometimes a word is borrowed and then shortened, so "football" becomes **le foot.** You'll find other examples of anglicisms in the notes on Language and Culture later in this chapter.

CONVERSATION 2

Richard est passé chez Aurélie, qui n'était pas chez elle.

RICHARD Je t'avais dit qu'elle **se paye ma tronche.** Ça fait un moment qu'elle me **mène en bateau.** Pas la peine de me **leurrer** je sens bien qu'elle **va me lâcher.**

AMER Là, tu **y vas un peu fort.** C'est quand même pas parce qu'elle manque un rencard qu'il faut en **faire tout un plat!** Toi, alors, t'as vraiment tendance à **broyer du noir!**

RICHARD Ces derniers temps je me suis **pris** pas mal **de vestes,** alors, ça s'expliquerait . . .

AMER **T'en fais pas.** Je suis sûr que tu te fais des idées. Rappelles-la, dis-lui tu lui apportes un truc extra qui va la **retaper.** Mets-y un brin d'humour. Si tu la fais **se marrer,** c'est gagné!

RICHARD Bon, OK, je l'appelle, mais j'ai l'impression que je vais me **prendre un râteau,** quelque chose de **mignon!**

ATTENTION AU LANGAGE FAMILER!

- **Elle se paye ma tronche:** See Chapitre 1, page 4, where you met the word **tronche** as a slang version of **visage.** You also met the expression **se payer une sale tronche** meaning "to look very rough." Here, **Elle se paye ma tronche** has the meaning of "She's jerking me around." ("She's winding me up." "She's having me on.")
- **Elle me mène en bateau:** literally, "She's taking me for a boat ride," meaning "She's leading me on." ("She's leading me up the garden path.")
- **se leurrer:** "to deceive yourself," "to fool yourself."
- **Elle va me lâcher:** "She's going to dump/drop me." "She's going to walk out on me."

Richard has called on Aurélie, who wasn't at home.

RICHARD I told you she was jerking me around (ripping the piss). She's been leading me on for quite a while now. No need to fool me. I can sense that she's going to ditch me.

AMER You're going a bit too far. Just because she misses a date, you don't have to make a big deal about it (a meal of it). You really do love to paint things as black as possible.

RICHARD I've taken a few knocks lately, which might explain things.

AMER Don't worry about it (go on about it). I'm sure that you're imagining things. Give her a call. Tell her you're going to bring her something to pick her up. Try to add a touch of wit. If you can get her to laugh, you've got it made (you're home and dry).

RICHARD OK, I'll give her a call, but I've got the feeling I'm going to get dumped. That *will* be nice, won't it!

- **Tu y vas un peu fort:** "You're laying it on a bit thick." "You're going a bit too far."
- **en faire tout un plat:** means to give an exaggerated importance to something, just like the British English expression "to make a meal of it." (American English: "to make a big deal of it.")
- **broyer du noir:** The verb **broyer** actually means "to grind," "to crush." So this expression means that you're so down in the dumps that you are crushing the black all around you.
- **prendre une veste:** means "to fall flat on your face" ("to come a cropper"). So when Richard says **ces derniers temps, je me suis pris pas mal de vestes,** he's telling us that he's taken quite a few knocks recently. Another expression using **veste** is **retourner sa veste.** It means "to change your opinion if it suits you to do so." Literally, the phrase has the same meaning as "turncoat."
- **T'en fais pas:** "Don't let it bother you." This is rather like **t'inquiète** explained in Chapitre 3, page 30.
- **retaper:** is often used with the meaning of "to fix up a house." When applied to a person it means "to lift somebody's spirits" ("to help somebody to buck up," "to give somebody a bit of a lift.")
- **se marrer:** means "to laugh," that is to say it can be used interchangeably with **rigoler.** Linked to **se marrer** is the commonly used adjective **marrant,** meaning "amusing."
- **prendre un râteau:** means much the same as **prendre une veste** but is used particularly for a relationship that breaks down, that is, **se faire lâcher,** "to be dropped," "to get the push."
- **mignon:** usually means "sweet," "cute." Here it is used ironically, because he's being dropped by his girlfriend. So it is like saying, "So that will be really nice!" with a heavy note of irony in your voice.

VOCABULAIRE DU CHAPITRE

assiette: dans son assiette	feeling good
la banlieue	suburbs
le/la beur	young Arab (*verlan*)
le bobard	lie, fib
booster	to give support, to make someone feel better
broyer du noir	to be down in the dumps, depressed
C'est vache!	That's terrible! That sucks! (That's a real pig!)
cassé	ill, unwell, totally exhausted
le céfran	français (*verlan*)
charrier	to push things too far, to exaggerate
chébran	branché (*verlan*)
choper la crève	to catch a chill
chouraver	to steal
comater	to be passed out, to be fast asleep
crever (de faim)	to die (of hunger)
dingue	crazy
en coup de vent	in a hurry
en faire tout un plat	to make a big deal about something (to make a meal of something)
le flic	cop, police
le fric	cash
le keuf	police (*verlan*)
le keus	bag (*verlan*)
lâcher	to leave
leurrer	to deceive
mener: Elle me mène en bateau.	She's taking me for a ride.
mignon	sweet, cute
le moral	morale

la nana	chick, girl (bird)
poser un lapin	to stand up, to leave in the lurch
prendre un râteau	to be dumped/dropped, to get the push
prendre une veste	to fall flat on your face (to come a cropper)
remonter le moral	to lift your spirits
retaper	to cheer someone up (to give someone a lift)
retourner sa veste	to change your ideas
le reub	Arab (*verlan*)
ripoux	rotten (*verlan*)
se faire lâcher	to get the push, to be dropped
se marrer	to laugh
se payer: Elle se paye ma tronche.	She's making fun of me (She's taking the piss).
sourdingue	deaf
T'en fais pas.	Don't go on about it. Don't let it bother you.
la tchatche	chatter, talk, language
la teuf	party (*verlan*)
tourner rond	to go well, to be successful
trouver une combine	to find a way around a problem
vache: C'est vache!	That's terrible. (That's a real pig.)
le verlan	backward language (See this chapter, page 67.)
y aller fort	to go over the top

À VOTRE TOUR!

A. Match the beginning of the idiom on the left to its correct ending on the right.

1. En faire tout un	a. crève
2. Passer en	b. en bateau
3. Broyer du	c. lapin
4. Choper la	d. plat
5. Raconter des	e. coup de vent
6. Ne pas avoir l'air	f. noir
7. Poser un	g. un râteau
8. Mener quelqu'un	h. bobards
9. Se prendre	i. dans son assiette

B. Match the French idiom on the left to its English equivalent on the right.

1. Choper la crève.	a. To poke fun at someone.
2. Y aller un peu fort.	b. To organize a party.
3. Manquer un rancard.	c. To overdo it/to exaggerate.
4. Trouver une combine.	d. To get a stinker of a cold.
5. Remonter le moral à quelqu'un.	e. To fall flat on your face. (To come a cropper.)
6. Faire une teuf.	f. To miss a date.
7. Ça va te retaper.	g. To think up a scam.
8. Prendre une veste.	h. To cheer someone up.
9. Se payer la tronche de quelqu'un.	i. It will pick you up.

C. In the following dialogue, replace the underlined, more formal expression by an appropriate colloquial idiom from the list:

lâcher	**le moral à zéro**	**chopé la crève**
était cassé	**mener en bateau**	**passait en coup de vent**
comater	**bobards**	**teuf**
m'a posé un lapin	**payé ma tronche**	

SANDRINE Salut Julie! Ça va?

JULIE Franchement non. <u>Je me sens déprimée</u> (1). Paul vient de <u>me quitter</u> (2).

SANDRINE Non! Quand est-ce que ça s'est passé?

JULIE Hier on devait aller à la soirée (3) de Luc. On avait rendez-vous à huit heures. Il n'est pas venu (4). J'y suis allée à pied. J'ai même attrapé froid (5). Une heure après, il est arrivé. Il a dit qu'il ne restait qu'une minute (6). Il m'a raconté des mensonges (7). Il devait, paraît-il, aller chercher Marc à la gare. Moi, je l'ai cru. Il s'est bien moqué de moi (8)!

SANDRINE C'est pas sympa! En fait, Marc n'était pas bien (9) et était resté se reposer (10) chez lui. Il aurait pu au moins te dire la vérité au lieu de te raconter toutes ces histoires (11)!

JULIE Après tout, il ne valait pas cher! Un de perdu dix de retrouvé. Vive la liberté!

D. What would you say in an informal situation? Try to use the expressions learned in this chapter.

1. J'ai poireauté dehors une heure hier. Il pleuvait des cordes. Ce matin, je ne me sens pas dans__________. J'ai dû choper __________.
2. C'est l'anniversaire d'Arnaud demain. On va lui organiser __________ sans qu'il le sache. Il fallait trouver __________ pour le faire sortir de chez lui. Armelle lui a raconté __________: des ouvriers qui doivent refaire le plancher! Ça nous donne une heure pour tout préparer!
3. Je viens de voir Sandrine. Elle a râté son examen et elle a le __________. C'est vraiment pas juste, en prendre seulement 12 sur les 190 qui se présentent! Ils __________ un peu fort.
4. On m'a fait venir à neuf heures du matin, posé des tas de questions: tout ça pour rien puisqu'ils avaient déjà choisi quelqu'un d'autre! On peut dire qu'ils se sont bien __________.
5. J'ai beau dire à Armelle que ça marche pas entre nous, on dirait qu'elle est __________. Elle veut rien comprendre. Elle va se __________. C'est clair!
6. Eric a toujours été plutôt pessimiste, je sais, mais là, vraiment ça s'arrange pas. Il arrête pas de __________. Le moindre petit problème, il en fait __________. J'ai peur qu'il nous fasse une vraie __________.

LANGUAGE AND CULTURE

ARGOT, VERLAN, AND LA LANGUE DES BANLIEUES

French, like all languages, is in a constant state of development and evolution. In this respect, the changes usually take place first of all in the spoken language, and it takes the written language time to catch up with the developments in speech. This is why the gap between spoken and written language may be considerable.

Nor can it be said that there is only a single version of the spoken language. An in-group may try to establish its own nonstandard forms of communication, which will be incomprehensible to outsiders. This is the way in which various forms of **argot** have developed over the years. Originally, **argot** was a jargon or code used by criminal classes, and involved using a particular vocabulary that was not known to the police or the respectable classes. **Argot** then came to mean any variety of nonstandard slang or jargon, particularly associated with the Parisian working class and sometimes proving to be very creative and inventive, especially in areas such as sex, drink, and money, and in activities of doubtful legality, such as drug-dealing, prostitution, and so on. Many of the "classic" words of **argot** have passed into daily language, words such as **les flics** (police); **le fric** (cash); **la bouffe** (food). Increasingly, largely because of the influence of films and TV, the barriers between **argot** and the standard spoken language have broken down. The recent development of argot has been marked by the speech patterns of **le parler jeune,** and, as the dialogues in this book show clearly, the spoken French of a wide variety of people, and especially young people, now draws freely on **argot.**

The growth and extension of **argot** and **verlan** have formed **la langue des banlieues.** The rapid growth of **les banlieues,** the vast outlying suburbs of major cities, has brought together large numbers of immigrants, largely Arab in origin but also from African countries. The language that has grown up here is closely linked to **la culture de banlieue,** a whole multicultural and multiracial phenomenon of modern France. A particular form of in-group language is **le verlan,** which began as a language game and acted as a sort of in-group code by reversing the order of syllables in a word. The word **verlan** itself is a reversed form of **l'envers,** meaning "back to front." Other examples include **céfran (français); chébran (branché); ripoux (pourri).** The ways in which this restricted code can be extended into society at large is made clear by such widely known titles as a song by Renaud, **Laisse béton (béton = tomber),** and the film ***Les Ripoux.*** **Verlan** has its own quite complex rules for word formation and may not offer only simple inversions like those given above. The word **sac** becomes **keus,** with a change of vowel, and the same is true of the word **teuf** used in this chapter to mean **fête. Femme** has been "verlanized" into **meuf,** which is in widespread use among young people, replacing the traditional **argot** word **nana.** Perhaps the most widely used **verlan** word in daily use is **beur** to mean "Arab," and formed from **arabe** via **beara** and finally **beur.** However, this also provides an example of another phenomenon. Clearly, a **verlan** word that is fully accepted has quite lost its "secret," rebellious quality, and may be replaced by a new invention or else "reverlanized." So **beur** has gone back through the same process to give a current form **reub.** Words from **argot** may themselves be "verlanized," for example, **flic** becomes **keuf,** now widely used for "police." **Verlan** is not a complete language but a way of giving new values to selected words.

Besides the widespread use of **argot** and **verlan, la tchatche (= la langue) de banlieue** is marked by numerous foreign borrowings, for example, **c'est kif kif** ("it's all the same"), **kiffant (chouette); chouffer (regarder)** from Arabic; **joint; sniffer; dealer** (from Anglo-American drug culture); **chouraver (voler)** from Romany. The different communities living in the **banlieues** have developed a sort of linguistic mosaic, drawing on a variety of linguistic traditions and blending them with French. But, although the words may have a clear foreign origin, they adapt to French rules of grammar. So verbs that have a clear English origin, such as **booster, blaster, shooter,** and **linker,** all take the appropriate verbal endings. They may, of course, also change their original meaning when used in French. So **linker** has the sense of "to seduce" as in **il a linké une meuf super.** The astonishing feature has been the speed with which many of these new creations have been taken over by the French younger generation, without any real distinctions of class. A whole series of books and articles have appeared to explain the language of the younger generation to their parents, for example, *Le vrai langage des jeunes expliqué aux parents* (E. Girard and B. Kernel, published by Albin Michel, 1997).

The nonnative speaker of French cannot really hope to keep up with the speed of such developments, and, as always, must be careful of which words to use in his/her own speech. But any acquaintance with student circles or other groups of younger people requires some understanding of the language use set out in this section. And in the final analysis, for anyone interested in the way French is developing, the explosive creativity of **la langue des banlieues** is a fascinating phenomenon.

. CHAPITRE 6 .

Alors, ça s'est bien passé? Tu as l'air fortement secoué! Ça me scie!

TELLING A STORY • EXPRESSING SURPRISE

CONVERSATION 1

Marc rentre de vacances et raconte à Éloïse ce qui est arrivé dans l'avion.

ÉLOÏSE Alors, ce voyage, ça c'est bien passé?

MARC Qu'est-ce qu'**on s'est marrés** avec Fred. Il y avait **un mec** qui **flippait à mort** à l'idée d'aller en avion. Il **s'était envoyé** trois whiskies **bien tassés** dans l'aéroport! Quand on est montés en avion, il était déjà **bourré.** Mais au bout d'une heure, on nous a dit de redescendre, parce qu'il y avait un **pépin** technique. Le **pauvre gars** avait continué à **picoler** sec pendant tout ce temps-là, alors il était **à l'ouest.** Il y comprenait **que dalle.** Y croyait **dur comme fer** qu'il était arrivé. Il **s'était collé** des lunettes de soleil et un chapeau de paille. Comme il faisait noir et qu'il était **beurré,** il **s'est cassé la gueule** dans la passerelle! J'te dis pas! Fred et moi **on se fendait la gueule!** Le mec, lui, il a rien senti: complètement anesthésié par l'alcool.

Marc has just gotten back from his vacation (holidays) and he tells Éloïse what happened on the plane.

Éloïse So, how was the trip? Did it go well?

Marc Me and Fred had a great laugh. There was this guy who was totally stressed out at the idea of flying. He threw back (had sunk) three very large whiskies. When we got on the plane he was already wasted (legless). An hour later they asked us to get off again because of some technical glitch (hitch). The poor fool (sod) had gone on hitting the bottle all that time, so he was all over the place, didn't have a clue. He was convinced that he'd arrived. He stuck on some shades and a straw hat. It was dark and he was plastered so he fell on his face on his way down the gangway. Fred and me burst out (creased up) laughing. The guy himself didn't feel a thing. He was completely anesthetized by the alcohol.

ATTENTION AU LANGAGE FAMILIER!

- **on s'est marrés:** In Chapitre 5 you learned that **se marrer** is one of the colloquial verbs for "to laugh." Later on in this dialogue you also have **On se fendait la gueule,** which means "We really fell down laughing." If you are really going to split your sides, you can use expressions like **se fendre la pêche** or **se tordre de rire.**
- **un mec:** still the most widely used colloquial word for "a guy," "a bloke." You can refer to **un brave mec** or **un sale mec,** and so on. When used by a woman (**mon mec**) it may be husband, lover, partner, or whatever is appropriate. An alternative with this meaning is **mon jules.**
- **flippait à mort:** The verb **flipper** has been borrowed from English with the sense here of "totally stressed out." You could also say **stressé à mort,** because the English *stress* has become common in French either as a noun or a verb. So you can say **c'est à cause du stress** or **ça me stresse.**
- **s'était envoyé:** The verb **s'envoyer** is used with the sense of "to sink/down a drink," **s'envoyer une boisson.** A quite different use of the verb is explained in the Language and Culture notes in Chapitre 7—**s'envoyer en l'air,** meaning "to make love."
- **bien tassés:** This is used here to mean "a really good-sized measure of drink." The phrase can be used in other situations to mean ". . . and the rest!" For example, **Elle a quarante ans bien tassés** means that she's probably more like forty-five.

CONVERSATION 2

Richard tombe sur Julien. Il vient de se faire ***raketter*** *et raconte sa mésaventure.*

RICHARD Dis donc, **mec,** tu as l'air fortement **secoué.** Qu'est-ce qui t'arrive?

JULIEN Je viens de me faire **dépouiller** par des **racailles!**

RICHARD J'y crois pas! en plein jour? **Tu délires!**

- **bourré:** one of the very many words for "drunk." Here are a few more variations: **être rond; être paf; être schlass; être beurré.** For someone who is paralytic, you can say **Il est complètement rétamé.** A more polite term for a woman who has had a drop too much is **Elle est un peu pompette.** Later in the dialogue is the verb **picoler,** meaning "to drink heavily," for which you could also use **siffler** or **écluser.**

- **pépin:** is a common word for a "hitch" or a "snag."

- **pauvre gars:** "poor fool" ("poor sod").

- **à l'ouest:** that is, he had no idea where he was; "all over the place."

- **que dalle:** very common expression for "zilch," "nothing at all" ("sod all"), for example, **J'y comprends que dalle,** "I don't understand a single word." Replacing **que dalle** in more up-to-date **argot** is **que tchi** (or **keutchi**), borrowed, apparently, from the Romany language.

- **Il croyait dur comme fer:** "He firmly believed."

- **Il s'était collé:** The verb **coller** means "to stick," so here he had "stuck on his shades." It is often used as a colloquial way to say **se mettre,** that is, "to put on (clothes, for example)."

- **Il s'est cassé la gueule:** In Chapitre 1 there were some notes on the meaning and use of **gueule.** This expression means "to fall flat on your face" ("to come a cropper") and is also found in the adjective **casse-gueule** meaning "dangerous," "risky." Even more violent is **se rétamer la gueule.**

Richard bumps into Julien. He has just been mugged and tells the story.

RICHARD What's up, buddy (mate)? You look really shaken up. What's happened?

JULIEN I've just been mugged by some scumbags (rogues).

RICHARD I can't believe it! In broad daylight! You're joking!

JULIEN Ils ont **déboulé** à trois d'un vieux van pourri. Le plus **baraqué** m'a dit: **«File-moi** ton blouson si tu veux pas que je te **défonce la face».** J'en **menais pas large,** je te le dis! J'avais aucune envie de me faire **buter.** Alors je me suis exécuté **rapido.**

RICHARD Et qu'est-ce qu'ils t'ont **piqué?**

JULIEN Ils m'ont **fauché** mes **fringues,** mon blouson, ma casquette, même mes **pompes!** J'ai eu **du bol** qu'ils me **tirent** pas mon **fute.**

RICHARD Incroyable! **Ça me scie** ça alors! Se faire **raketter** en pleine ville en plus!

JULIEN Je peux te dire qu'ils ont pas **chômé.** Des vrais **pro,** en cinq minutes c'était **réglé! Ni vu ni connu!** Je me suis retrouvé sur le trottoir, en chaussettes!

RICHARD Allez, viens. Je t'emmène prendre **un bock,** t'en as besoin, **c'est clair.**

ATTENTION AU LANGAGE FAMILIER!

- **raketter:** The word **racket** has been borrowed from English to mean any sort of dishonest scheme. Here, the verb means to be "mugged" ("done over").
- **mec:** Here **mec** is used as a friendly form of address: "buddy" ("mate").
- **secoué:** "all shaken up."
- **dépouiller:** "to strip off," so with the meaning here of "to rob," "to clean out."
- **racaille:** "rabble," "riffraff," "scum."
- **Tu délires!** "You've got to be joking." "You can't be serious."
- **déboulé:** means "to arrive quite unexpectedly," "to turn up suddenly."
- **baraqué:** used to describe a heavily built, muscular type.

Julien There were three of them. They sprang out from an old rotting van. The biggest thug said, "Just hand me your jacket, and make it quick or I'll kick your face in." I didn't make (kick up) a stink, I can tell you. I didn't want to get myself taken out. So I did what he said pronto.

Richard What did they rip off (nick)?

Julien They swiped my gear (dregs); my jacket, my cap, even my shoes (deeks). I was lucky they didn't take my pants (strides).

Richard I can't believe it! I'm shocked (gobsmacked)! To be mugged in broad daylight!

Julien Believe me, they didn't linger. They were real pros. It was over (sorted) in five minutes. Incognito. I was left there on the pavement in my socks.

Richard Come on. I'll treat you to a brew (bevy). I can see you need one for sure.

- **file-moi:** "Give me . . ." (see Chapitre 4, page 42).
- **défonce la face:** "smash your face in."
- **Je n'en menais pas large:** This means something like "My stomach was all in knots." ("My heart was in my boots.")
- **buter:** means "to kill" (usually violently).
- **rapido:** is a colloquial form of **rapidement.**
- **piquer** and **faucher:** are both used with the sense of "to steal." Note that the literal meaning of **faucher** is "to mow" or "to scythe" (from **la faux** "scythe"). So you can see how it comes to mean "steal," and also why it is used in the expression **fauché comme les blés.** This is literally "cut down like wheat" and is used colloquially to mean "totally broke" ("completely skint").
- **fringues:** is a standard, colloquial term for "clothes." There is also a verb **se fringuer,** meaning "to get dressed up," as in **Vise un peu comme elle est fringuée!** "Just take a look at what she's wearing!" Among your clothes you then have **pompes** ("shoes," often "sports shoes") or **godasses,** a more general word for any sort of footwear.
- **avoir du bol:** "to be in luck." This might also be **avoir du pot.**
- **Ils me tirent mon fute:** "They take my trousers/slacks/pants (strides)."
- **Ça me scie:** Richard is quite literally cut up about it! This means "That saws me in half."
- **chômé:** The verb **chômer** means "to be out of work." A day without work is **un jour chômé.** Therefore, it has the sense of "to have time on your hands." So here he is saying, "They didn't hang around (about)."
- **des vrais pro:** "real professionals."
- **régler:** means "to settle up," for example, **régler le compte** is to "settle the bill." So here it means everything was finished, tied up, done with.

- **Ni vu ni connu!** "You wouldn't even guess anything had happened!"
- **un bock:** "a glass of beer," "a drink" ("a bevy").
- **C'est clair:** "That's for sure."

VOCABULAIRE DU CHAPITRE

à l'ouest	completely lost
aveugle	blind
avoir du bol	to be in luck
avoir du pot	to be in luck
baraqué	heavily built, muscular
bien tassé (un whisky)	a good measure (of whisky)
un bock	a glass of beer, a drink, a brew (a bevy)
bourré	drunk
Les bras m'en sont tombés.	I was absolutely amazed.
buter	to kill
C'est clair.	That's for sure.
Ça me scie.	I'm really shocked. (literally: "That saws me in half.")
chômer	to be out of work, to hang around (about)
coller	to stick
croire dur comme fer	to be absolutely convinced
débouler	to turn up quite unexpectedly
défoncer	to smash in
dépouiller	to strip off
faucher	to steal, to rob (to nick)
filer	to give
flipper (à mort)	to get (totally) stressed out
le fric	cash
les fringues	clothes
la fute	trousers, slacks, pants (strides)

les godasses	shoes, footwear
le jules	man, lover, partner, husband
manchot	one-armed (or, sometimes, without arms)
le mec	guy (bloke)
mener: Je n'en menais pas large.	My stomach was all in knots. (My heart was in my boots.)
Ni vu ni connu!	You wouldn't even know anything had happened!
pauvre gars	poor fool (poor sod)
le pépin	glitch, hitch, snag
piquer	to steal (to nick)
les pompes	shoes, sports shoes
le/la pro	professional
que dalle	zilch, nothing at all (sod all)
que tchi (keutchi)	nothing (sod all)
la racaille	rabble, riffraff, scum
raketter	to mug (to do over)
rapido	fast
régler	to settle up, to finish up
s'envoyer en l'air	to make love
s'envoyer	down a drink (to sink)
se casser la gueule*	to fall flat on your face (to come a cropper)
se fendre la gueule*	to split your sides laughing
se fendre la pêche	to fall down (about) laughing
se fringuer	to get dressed up
se marrer	to laugh
se rétamer la gueule	to fall flat on your face (to come a cropper)
se tordre de rire	to fall down laughing, to split your sides
secouer	to shake up
stressé (à mort)	(totally) stressed out
suer	to sweat
Tu délires!	You've got to be joking! You can't be serious!

À VOTRE TOUR!

A. Complete the expressions on the left. Then match them to the English equivalent on the right.

1. Le mec était à __________.
2. Des racailles ont tout à coup __________ d'une voiture.
3. Je viens de me faire ________ mon porte-monnaie.
4. On n'a pas __________, j'peux te le dire.
5. C'est la deuxième fois que je me fais __________ dans ce quartier.
6. J'y comprends que ________ à son histoire.
7. Après ses trois whiskies, il était complètement __________.
8. Quand il les a vus, il a commencé à __________.

a. My wallet has just been ripped off (nicked).
b. I can tell you we didn't take long.
c. When he saw them, he was dead scared.
d. I understand zilch (bugger-all) in his story.
e. After his third scotch, he was really pissed.
f. The guy was all over the place.
g. Some thugs piled out of a car.
h. It's the second time I've been mugged in this area.

B. Match the synonyms. Match the colloquial expression on the left to the more formal equivalent on the right. (Two of the colloquial expressions have the same meaning.)

1. Il était bourré.
2. Il s'est cassé la gueule.
3. Il a fauché.
4. Il a déboulé.
5. Il a du bol.
6. Il se fendait la gueule.
7. Il était à l'ouest.
8. Il s'est envoyé.
9. Il a paumé ses fringues.

a. Il a de la chance.
b. Il est arrivé sans prévenir.
c. Il était saoûl.
d. Il est tombé.
e. Il a perdu ses vêtements.
f. Il riait beaucoup.
g. Il a volé.
h. Il a bu.

C. What should you say in the following situation?

a. You are talking to an older person:

1. Tell her you fell in the street. ____________________
2. Tell her the passersby just laughed. ____________________
3. Tell her someone stole your wallet. ____________________
4. Tell her how unlucky you've been. ____________________

b. You are now talking to a student friend of yours.

1. Tell him you fell in the street. ____________________
2. Tell him the passersby just laughed.____________________
3. Tell him someone stole your wallet.____________________
4. Tell him how unlucky you've been.____________________

D. Complete the sentences according to context using the phrases below.

flipper à mort	**défoncer**	**buter**	**piquer**
racailles	**files**	**dépouillé**	**caisse**
pas large	**que dalle**	**baraqués**	

CHRISTOPHE Allô, Vincent? C'est Christophe. On vient de me (1) ____________ mes affaires. Juste à la sortie du stade!

VINCENT Mais t'es où là? T'as l'air de (2)____________.

CHRISTOPHE Je t'appelle d'une cabine. J'suis rue San Antonio. D'ici je peux voir les (3) ____________ qui m'ont (4) ____________. Ils sont deux et plutôt (5) ____________!

VINCENT Écoute, j'comprends (6) ____________ à ton histoire, et en plus la ligne est pas très bonne. Tu veux que je vienne te chercher avec ma (7) ____________ c'est ça?

CHRISTOPHE Oui, s'il te plaît, mais fais vite. S'ils me voient ils vont me (8) ____________ la face. J'en mène (9) ____________, j'te l'dis!

VINCENT Calme-toi, vieux, je fais au plus vite. T'as bien des thunes sur toi? Si tu leur (10) ____________ ton fric, ils vont pas te (11) ____________.

CHRISTOPHE	Facile à dire! Mais j'aimerais mieux pas me retrouver encore face à face avec eux. J't'attends, je bouge pas. Fais vite.
VINCENT	OK, j'arrive!

HISTOIRES DRÔLES

— Mais je vous reconnais, vous! La semaine dernière vous étiez aveugle et aujourd'hui vous êtes **manchot!**
— Eh oui, ma petite dame! J'ai recouvré la vue et **les bras m'en sont tombés!**

"I recognize you! Last week you were blind and this week you've got no arms!"

"Yes, that's the way it is, lady. My sight came back and I was completely bowled over."

(Here the play on words is with the expression **les bras m'en sont tombés,** meaning, "I was absolutely amazed!" as well as its literal meaning.)

*****

— Moi, les femmes, **je les fais suer,** puis je leur prends leur **fric.**
— C'est pas très correct ça!
— Comment pas très correct? Qu'est-ce qu'il y a de mal à tenir un club de gym?

"Well, you know what I do with women? I make them sweat and then I take their money."

"That's not a very nice way to behave."

"What d'you mean, not a nice way to behave? What's wrong with running a health club?"

. CHAPITRE 7 .

Entre nous deux, c'est cool. J'suis raide dingue de toi. Il est franchement craquant!

EXPRESSING YOUR FEELINGS
•
USING EXPRESSIONS OF LOVE AND AFFECTION

CONVERSATION 1

Émilie et Guillaume se disputent à la porte d'une disco.

GUILLAUME Mais enfin, qu'est-ce que t'as? **Y en a marre** de te voir **tirer la gueule** dans ton coin!

ÉMILIE Eh bien, toi, t'as un sacré **culot!** On sort **en boîte** ensemble et t'arrêtes pas de **mater** la nana là-bas et de la **baratiner** toute la soirée. Tu crois pas que **tu pousses** un peu?

GUILLAUME Écoute, tu vas pas me **faire une scène!** T'es complètement **à côté de la plaque!** C'est Cécile, une vieille copine de classe, figure-toi, et je ne l'avais pas vue depuis **un bail.**

IL A BARATINÉ CETTE NANA TOUTE LA SOIRÉE.

Émilie and Guillaume are having a fight outside a disco.

GUILLAUME Hey, come on, what's with (niggling) you? I'm fed up with seeing you pouting (pull a face) in your little corner.

ÉMILIE Oh, really, well you've got a hell of a lot of nerve (one hell of a cheek), I must say. We go clubbing together and you don't stop eyeing up the chick (bird) over there and you spend all evening hitting on her (chatting her up). Don't you think you're pushing it?

GUILLAUME Oh come on, don't make a scene (cause a stink)! You're off the wall. Look, that's just Cécile, an old school friend, and I haven't seen her for ages (yonks).

ÉMILIE Tu crois sans doute que je vais **gober** ton histoire?

GUILLAUME Émilie, arrête. **Te monte pas la tête.** Entre nous deux, c'est **cool,** et en plus **c'est du solide.** Tu sais bien que tu me plais. J'ai vraiment un gros **faible** pour toi. S'il te plaît, fais-moi confiance! Me **lâche** pas. J'suis **raide dingue** de toi.

ATTENTION AU LANGAGE FAMILIER!

- **Y en a marre:** short for **il y en a marre** or Guillaume might say, **J'en ai marre,** meaning "I've had enough . . ."; "I'm sick to death of. . . ."
- **tirer la gueule:** We've already met a number of expressions using **gueule.** This one means "to pout" ("to pull a face").
- **culot:** This is "cheek." You can say, as here, **Tu as un sacré culot,** or **Tu es drôlement culotté,** "You've got a hell of a lot of nerve." ("You've got one hell of a cheek.") Instead of **culotté** you can use **gonflé** with the same sense.
- **en boîte:** "a club" is **une boîte,** so **sortir en boîte** is "to go clubbing."
- **mater:** This can just mean "to look at," but usually it has the sense of "eyeing up" a member of the opposite sex.
- **baratiner:** "to hit on" ("to chat up").
- **tu pousses:** "You're pushing it." "You're going too far."
- **faire une scène:** just like the English "make a scene."
- **à côté de la plaque:** when you've got something completely wrong; to get completely the wrong idea.
- **depuis un bail:** "for ages" ("for yonks").
- **gober:** This verb means "to swallow whole," like when you're eating oysters. From that it has come to mean "to swallow an unlikely story."

ÉMILIE I suppose you think I'm going to fall for that story?

GUILLAUME Émilie, stop. Don't blow your top. It's cool between us, and solid as well. You know how much I like you. I've really got a soft spot for you. Please, just trust me. Don't ditch me. I'm crazy (fruit loopy) about you.

- **Te monte pas la tête:** "Don't go over the top." "Don't blow your top."
- **cool:** borrowed from American English with all its range of meanings.
- **c'est du solide; avoir un faible; lâcher; raide dingue:** For all these expressions, see the section on Language and Culture at the end of the chapter.

(See Conversation 2.)

CONVERSATION 2

Juliette parle à sa mère de son petit ami Stéphane.

JULIETTE Alors, il est super, non?

MÈRE Et bien, oui, oui, il a l'air gentil.

JULIETTE Gentil? Mais il est adorable. Quand il sourit, avec ses fossettes, il est franchement **craquant,** non? D'ailleurs, **j'ai flashé** sur lui dès que l'ai vu. De corps c'est peut-être pas le genre **tablettes de chocolat,** mais il me plaît comme il est . . .

MÈRE Mais est-ce qu'il est intéressant? Quand je l'ai vu il n'a pratiquement pas ouvert la bouche, alors. . . .

JULIETTE Normal! Il te connaît pas. C'est pas le genre à **baratiner.** Mais crois-moi, entre copains, c'est un marrant. Quand il raconte des histoires, tout le monde est **plié de rire!**

MÈRE Est-ce que tu crois que c'est **du sérieux?**

JULIETTE Tu sais avec lui, ça s'explique pas. Je me sens **hyper** bien. On aime les mêmes trucs, on **s'éclate** vraiment quand on est ensemble. **Je ne fais pas de films,** mais je crois que cette fois, je suis plutôt **accro** . . . !

ATTENTION AU LANGAGE FAMILIER!

- **C'est du sérieux:** "It's the real thing this time."
- **craquant:** What's your favorite word to describe the man or woman you love? Whatever it is in English, here's what you say in French.
- **J'ai flashé:** "I was in love at first sight."
- **des tablettes de chocolat:** This is a reference to "abs," abdominal muscles, also called "a six-pack." Used to refer to a

---

Juliette chats to her mother about her friend Stéphane.

JULIETTE So, he's great, isn't he?

MOTHER Well, yes, he seems very nice.

JULIETTE Nice! He's gorgeous! When he smiles, with those dimples, well he's really hot (dishy), don't you think? Anyway, I fell head over heels as soon as I saw him. I suppose his body isn't exactly Adonis, but I like him the way he is.

MOTHER But is he interesting? When I saw him he hardly opened his mouth.

JULIETTE That's because he doesn't know you. That's what you'd expect. He's not the smooth-talking type. But you can take my word for it, when he's with his friends (mates), he's a real laugh. When he tells stories, everybody cracks up (wets themselves laughing).

MOTHER And do you think it is going to last with him? Do you think it's serious?

JULIETTE You see, I can't explain it. I just feel hot when I'm with him. We like the same sort of things. We really hit it off (get on like a house on fire) when we're together. I'm not imagining this (glamming it up), but I reckon this time I'm really hooked.

---

splendid physical specimen, for example, **Il a drôlement la tablette de chocolat, le mec.**

- **plié de rire:** This has the same meaning as **tordre de rire,** "to fall down laughing." (See Chapitre 6, page 72.)
- **hyper:** can be added onto an adjective to add to its force and intensity.
- **on s'éclate:** a way of saying that you really hit it off together.

- **Je ne fais pas de films:** She really means it, she's not "inventing some story" ("glamming it up"). She doesn't have any illusions. This is the real thing.
- **accro:** derived from **accroché,** "hooked." It is also used of someone who is hooked on drugs.

VOCABULAIRE DU CHAPITRE

à côté de la plaque	way off the mark
accro	hooked
le bail	long time, age
le baiser	kiss
baiser*	to fuck
baratiner	to hit on (to chat up)
la boîte	club
C'est du sérieux.	It's really serious.
le câlin	cuddle, caress
chialer*	to weep, to cry
la cohabitation	living together
la compagne	partner (female)
le compagnon	partner (male)
cool	cool
coucher avec	to bed, to sleep with
craquant	gorgeous
le culot	cheek
culotté, être	to have a lot of nerve (cheek)
dingue	crazy
la drague	hitting on (chatting up)
draguer	to pick up, to hit on (to chat up)
emballer	to pick up
le faible	weak spot

faire des films	to invent a drama
faire une scène	to create a scene
flasher	to spark, to fall head over heels
gaulois	bawdy
gober	to swallow whole
gonflé, être	to have a lot of nerve (cheek)
hyper bien	couldn't be better
jouir	to come, to hit the heights (sexually)
lâcher	to leave, to drop someone
marre: en avoir marre	to be fed up with
mater	to eye up
monter la tête	to get angry, mad
pacser	See the Language and Culture section in this chapter, page 95.
peloter	to touch up
pied: C'est le pied!	It's absolutely the best!
plier de rire	to wet yourself laughing (to crease yourself)
pousser	to push (too far)
prendre son pied	to have a lot of fun
raide dingue (de quelqu'un)	crazy (about somebody)
s'éclater	to hit it off together
sauter une fille/un mec	to lay a girl/guy
solide: C'est du solide.	It's something solid, durable.
les tablettes de chocolat	"abs," six-pack
tirer la gueule*	to pout (to pull a face)

À VOTRE TOUR!

A. Fill in the word that is missing from each phrase, using one of the words from the list:

solide	**marre**	**baratiner**	**faible**
lâche	**bail**	**craquant**	**films**

1. Depuis une heure tu ne me parle que de cette soirée. Je commence à en avoir ___________.
2. Il est tout le temps avec Armelle. C'est clair qu'il a vraiment un gros ___________ pour elle.
3. C'est une amie. Ça faisait un___________ que je ne l'avais pas vue.
4. Tu connais Julien? Moi, je dois dire que je le trouve franchement ___________.
5. Lui, il est plutôt du genre timide. C'est pas son truc de ________________ .
6. Tu veux savoir si ça va durer entre nous? Je ne sais pas. Je ne me fais pas de _________ , on verra bien.
7. Entre nous deux ça fait déjà un moment que ça dure. C'est du ______________.
8. Écoute, ne te mets pas en colère pour rien. Je t'en prie, ne me ___________ pas!

B. Choose the response that best gives the real meaning of the following underlined idioms.

1. <u>Il a un sacré culot.</u>
   a. Il a beaucoup de chance.
   b. Il est effronté.

2. Elle ne peut pas <u>gober</u> ton histoire.
   a. être d'accord avec
   b. croire

3. Elle <u>mate</u> tous les mecs qui passent.
   a. regarde bien
   b. critique méchamment

4. Il admet qu'il a flashé tout de suite sur elle.
   a. a été attiré au premier regard
   b. est tombé fou amoureux

5. Je suis maintenant totalement accro.
   a. Je ne peux plus m'en passer.
   b. Je suis désespéré.

6. Il est raide dingue de cette fille.
   a. fou amoureux
   b. très jaloux

7. Il a maintenant les tablettes de chocolat.
   a. des muscles bien développés.
   b. la super forme.

8. Je sens qu'elle va me faire une scène.
   a. tout faire pour se faire pardonner.
   b. me faire toutes sortes de reproches.

C. Complete the expressions on the left, and then match them to the English equivalents on the right.

1. Arrête de ________!
2. Elle est tout à fait __________.
3. Tu crois pas que tu __________.
4. Tu ne vas pas__________.
5. Ça fait __________ que je ne l'ai pas vu.
6. Toi, alors, t'as un __________!
7. On était tous __________.
8. Ensemble, on __________.

a. We all fell down laughing.
b. You've got a hell of a lot of nerve (one hell of a cheek)!
c. I haven't seen him for ages!
d. We hit it off when we are together.
e. Aren't you pushing your luck a bit far?
f. Don't throw a fit!
g. She's got it all wrong.
h. Stop looking as black as thunder!

D. Follow the instructions, using expressions from this chapter.

1. Tell him to stop eyeing up the chick (the bird) over there.

   ____

2. Ask her to keep her cool.

   ____

3. Suggest that you go clubbing together.

   ____

4. Tell your friend you've really got the hots for her.

   ____

5. Tell your friend that he turned you on as soon as you saw him.

   ____

6. Say that you are really hooked.

   ____

7. Tell her that the relationship you have together is serious.

   ____

LANGUAGE AND CULTURE

LOVE, SEX, AND TOGETHERNESS

A glance at the magazines on a newsrack or at the visual and verbal ingenuity of the advertising industry will show that the French have enthusiastically embraced the permissive society and the freedom of expression it allows. But these are just modern manifestations of an older truth, that the French enjoy sex and have always been more happily tolerant of young lovers, extramarital liaisons, and all those pleasures that have been frowned on and excluded by more puritanical and more hypocritical societies. The interest and humor generated by sex is shown, for example, in the songs of Georges Brassens, who sings sympathetically of **la première fille qu'on a pris dans ses bras,** who stands up for unfaithful wives (**Ne jetez pas la pierre à la femme adultère, Je suis derrière**), and who still has an erection when he thinks of his former lover Fernande (**quand je pense à Fernande, je bande, je bande**). Brassens died in 1981, but it is still impossible to imagine many of his songs being sung in English.

Looking back in time one might ask where in the English literature of the nineteenth century there is any treatment of an adulterous wife to compare with *Madame Bovary* (Flaubert), of a sexual and social climber like *Bel Ami* (Maupassant), or of anything to approach Zola's concern with sexuality in a novel such as *Nana*. One could look further back in history to *Les Blasons du Corps Féminin* of the sixteenth century, lovingly and poetically dwelling on each delight of the female body. And it must surely be historical evidence that the adjective **gaulois,** referring to the country of Gaul which was invaded by the Romans, has come to mean a bawdy or "gallic" humor. The Hachette dictionary gives two main meanings for **gaulois:** *1. Caractéristique de la France, de ses traditions; 2. Qui a la gaieté un peu libre du "bon vieux temps."*

So, as you would expect, the colloquial (and vulgar) language is full of imaginative and creative ways of talking about sex, love, the body, and relationships. If we begin at the beginning, we have **la drague** and the verb **draguer,** meaning "picking up." So you might say of a friend who was particularly focused on extending the range of his female acquaintances, **Il ne pense qu'à la drague** or **Il est un peu dragueur.** Of course, with equality of the sexes now a fact, it is just as likely that a woman will **draguer un mec.** The same meaning is conveyed by **emballer.** You may start by eyeing up (**mater**) the prey, and part of your technique will certainly include a little **baratin,** that's your technique for hitting on (chatting up) (**baratiner**). If your **drague** is successful, you will have your **mec** or **jules** (if you are a woman) or your **nana** (if you are a man). Note that gay couples use the same vocabulary, so a gay man will refer to his partner as **mon mec.** You are in love, so you can use terms like **être dingue de quelqu'un** ("to be mad about someone") or **avoir un gros faible pour quelqu'un** ("to have a real soft spot for someone"). Perhaps you might try a few caresses. **Un petit câlin** might be just a "nice cuddle," but **un câlin** can also have more erotic overtones. More precise is **peloter,** meaning "to caress a girl," particularly her breasts.

You will end up in bed, and **coucher avec quelqu'un** can only mean one thing, **faire l'amour,** or, more colloquially, **s'envoyer en l'air.** If you're lucky, you'll hit the heights, **jouir** or **prendre son pied.** This latter phrase can apply to making love or to almost any pleasure. Compare it with the idiom **C'est le pied!** or **C'est le super pied,** meaning "It was absolutely the greatest imaginable." Here you must know one of the great ambiguities of the French language. Although the noun **un baiser** means "a kiss," the verb **baiser** means "to fuck," unless it has something else following, such as **baiser la main de quelqu'un,** "to kiss someone's hand." If you want a verb for "to kiss" you must use **embrasser** or **se faire la bise.** You might use **se rouler un patin** or **se rouler des pelles.** For getting someone into bed you can choose from **s'envoyer une fille/un mec; se taper une fille/un mec;** or **se faire une fille/un mec.** For a while you'll be **accro,** you will have something that's really going to last (**c'est du solide**) but maybe things will grow cool. Perhaps one will start to bore the other, in which case **Il/elle me casse les pieds** or **Il/elle me prend la tête,** or **Il/elle me gonfle.** With the same meaning, but rather more vulgar, is **Il/elle me fait chier.** It may all end in tears, with one weeping (**chialer**) or yelling at the other (**engueuler**). Eventually, one will make the decision to drop (**lâcher** or **plâquer**) the other. If you have suffered such a disappointment in love, you might describe it as **prendre un râteau,** or **prendre une veste.**

After this rather swift affair (**aventure**), we should just dwell on longer relationships. Changing social circumstances means that the language has to adapt to the idea of long-term unmarried partners. In the 1950s and 1960s, marriage was still the popular option. By the 1990s, more than 15 percent of couples living together were in a **union libre,** and the great majority of married couples begin by living together first (**cohabitation**). So **les couples cohabitants** need a word equivalent to the English "partner," and they refer to **mon compagnon** or **ma compagne.** The social circumstances and the language have again been changed by a significant law passed in 1999, referred to as the **PACS (Pacte civil de solidarité).** This gave equal rights in law to any couple choosing to live together, whether gay, straight, or in any other relationship. Such a union can be formally recognized by a tribunal, but since this cannot be described as a marriage, the verb **pacser** has entered the language.

. CHAPITRE 8 .

C'est toujours hyper-bondé; grand comme un mouchoir de poche; une meuf aguichante et marrante

DESCRIBING PLACES
•
DESCRIBING PEOPLE

CONVERSATION 1

Aurélie et Éloïse essaient de se mettre d'accord pour choisir un endroit où passer la nouvelle année avec leurs copains.

AURÉLIE Tu te rappelles le dîner au resto l'an dernier! Qui avait **dégoté** cette adresse de resto **guindé** et **tape-à-l'oeil? Pour l'ambiance, bonjour!** Tous ces mecs qui pensaient qu'à **s'empiffrer** en silence! On s'est fait **chier** toute la soirée!

ÉLOÏSE Qu'est-ce qu'on **foutait** là! Bon, ce sera pas difficile de **se concocter** un meilleur **plan** cette année. J'ai pensé au Bistro des Arts. C'est dans un coin un peu **glauque,** mais c'est super à l'intérieur; décor rétro, petites lampes tamisées et l'ambiance est très **décontract.**

Aurélie and Éloïse are trying to agree on a place where they can spend New Year's Eve with their friends.

AURÉLIE D'you remember last year's dinner in the restaurant? Who on earth dug up the name of that swanky place? Talk about atmosphere! Forget it! All those guys just concentrating on pigging out in silence. The whole evening was the absolute pits.

ÉLOÏSE Why on earth were we hanging around (messing about at going) there? Anyway, it shouldn't be difficult to cook up a better plan this year. I was wondering about the Bistro des Arts. It's in kind of a shitty area, but inside it's great. The décor's got some period flavor, you know, little shaded lights and a really chilled-out atmosphere.

AURÉLIE Le problème, c'est que c'est un peu **crade** là-dedans. En cuisine ça doit être carrément **dégueu.** En plus, c'est toujours **hyper-bondé,** et dans un **boucan** d'enfer comme ça, on s'entend pas.

ÉLOÏSE J'ai une idée! **L'appart** de Guillaume, grand comme **un mouchoir de poche,** peut-être, mais vraiment très sympa. On **se ramène** tous et on s'y cuisine une bonne petite **bouffe.**

AURÉLIE Toi, t'es **gonflée** alors! J'imagine la tronche qu'il va tirer quand tu vas lui annoncer ça!

ATTENTION AU LANGAGE FAMILIER!

- **dégoter:** means the same as **trouver.** It usually means "finding something after looking quite carefully."
- **guindé:** "stiff," "starchy," "uptight."
- **tape-à-l'oeil:** "tacky." Literally it means something like "trying to hit you right between the eyes."
- **Pour l'ambiance, bonjour!** This is equivalent to the use in English of "hello" as an exclamation. Nothing at all to do with greeting somebody, it's used ironically to express a judgment, "As far as atmosphere is concerned, forget it!" You might, for example, say, **J'ai retrouvé un job, mais alors, bonjour la galère,** meaning "I've managed to get a new job, but what a load of work!" The expression was popularized in a famous antialcohol campaign in the 1980s: **Un verre, ça va. Trois verres, bonjour les dégâts!** "One glass, OK. Three glasses, just watch out for the damage!"
- **s'empiffrer:** "to stuff your face."
- **on s'est fait chier*:** Even as recently as the 1970s, **chier** ("to shit") was a taboo word, too vulgar to use in normal conversation. Now it occurs in all sorts of quite common expressions, such as here, where it means "We were bored out of our minds," and in

AURÉLIE The only problem is it's a bit filthy (a bit of a mucky place). In the kitchen it must be really gross. Anyway, it's always totally crowded (heaving), and in a hell of a racket like that, you can't hear yourself speak.

ÉLOÏSE I've got an idea! Guillaume's apartment (flat). It's small (minute), maybe, but it's a really nice place. If we all turn up together there we could fix ourselves a good little meal (nosh-up).

AURÉLIE You've got a hell of a lot of nerve (cheek)! Just imagine his face when we tell him!

---

the phrase **en chier**, for example, **J'en ai chié pour gagner ce match,** which means "I really had to bust a gut to win the match." The adjective **chiant** ("boring") is also used and the noun **chierie** to mean "something very tedious," **quelle chierie tout ce travail!**

- **foutait:** See the discussion of the verb **foutre** in Chapitre 2.
- **se concocter un plan:** to concoct or hatch a plan
- **un endroit glauque:** The original meaning of **glauque** was to refer to a color, a sort of dull blue-green. Now the word has a new lease on life in popular speech to mean a rather dubious, shady sort of place. A French word with a smiliar meaning is **louche.**
- **décontract:** "chilled-out"; "mellow." This is a short form of **décontracté,** and it's worth noting that French has a strong tendency to shorten words. In this dialogue you also have **dégueu** for **dégueulasse*** ("disgusting") and **appart** for **appartement.**
- **crade:** This is one of a family of words that probably started with **crasseux,** meaning "filthy." **Crade** is a short form of **cradingue** and may also appear as **crado, crados,** or **craspec.** The addition of **s** to form **crados** is typical of a tendency to add an **s** where it's not really needed; for example, **rapidos** instead of **rapido.** The word **cassos** (from **se casser**) means "Let's go," in other words, the same as **on se tire.**

- **hyper-bondé:** In Chapitre 7, the point was made that **hyper** can be added to an adjective to reinforce it. So **hyper bien** was "really well" and **hyper-bondé** is "so packed you couldn't get another person into the place."
- **boucan d'enfer:** "a hell of a racket."
- **(petit comme) un mouchoir de poche:** no bigger than a pocket handkerchief.
- **se ramène:** "all get together"
- **bouffe:** "grub," fodder (nosh). Note how often the French use **petit** when talking about things they like: **une bonne petite bouffe et un bon petit vin dans un petit resto quelque part.**
- **t'es gonflé:** means the same as **t'es culotté,** "You've got a hell of a lot of nerve (cheek)."

CONVERSATION 2

Amer et Richard font des études de média et doivent présenter une vidéo. Ils cherchent des étudiants-acteurs pour leur film.

AMER Bon, alors pour la présentatrice, on a Monique: belle **gueule,** assez **bourge,** et en plus, elle **passe bien,** je trouve. Et toi?

RICHARD D'accord. Pour le voyageur on a Paul. T'as dû le voir: il est toujours **fourré** à la cafétéria. C'est un type plutôt **rigolard,** avec une barbe et des petits **binocles** ronds . . . souvent **un peu bourré.**

AMER Ah, oui, je vois qui c'est. C'est l**e mec** qui a toujours **un fute** vert et un viel imper **crade? Bof . . . Pas génial** je trouve. Moi, je verrais plutôt le grand, avec un air toujours un peu **largué.** Tu vois qui?

RICHARD Mais oui, Marlot, Stéphane Marlot. Lui, il est plutôt **je-m'en-foutiste.** Ça sera pas **du gâteau** d'arriver à le **mettre dans le coup.**

C'EST UN MEC QUI A TOUJOURS L'AIR UN PEU LARGUÉ.

Amer and Richard are doing media studies and they have to present a video. They are looking for students to act in their film.

AMER OK, right, for the presenter we've got Monique. Good looker, bit classy. Anyway, I think she's great on film. What do you say?

RICHARD Yes, sure, no problem. For the part of the traveler we've got Paul. You must have seen him. He's always hanging out (holed up) in the cafeteria. He's kind of a joker with a beard and John Lennon specs. Often half gone.

AMER Right, I've got him now. It's the guy who's always wearing green slacks and a grubby old raincoat (mac). I don't think much of that idea. I'd rather go for the tall guy always looking a bit spaced out. Do you know who I mean?

RICHARD Of course, Stéphane Marlot. He doesn't give a shit (a toss) about anything. It won't be a piece of cake to put him in the picture.

AMER Pour **la nana** de Paul, maintenant voyons qui on a? Il nous faut une **meuf** bien **foutue, aguichante,** et **marrante** en plus.

RICHARD **Te prends plus la tête.** Stéphanie est **partante.** J'lui en ai déjà parlé.

ATTENTION AU LANGAGE FAMILIER!

- **gueule:** This word has appeared a few times in the book, with various uses. Here **belle gueule** is referring to Monique's good looks. The exact meaning of the expression is that she has "a good bone structure," "fine features." See also Chapitre 1, page 4.
- **bourge:** short for **bourgeois,** "She's got a bit of class." ("She's a bit of a sloane.")
- **Elle passe bien:** "She's good in photos/in film."
- **fourré**: hanging out ("holed up").
- **rigolard:** from **rigoler,** "to laugh." He's a bit of a joker.
- **binocles:** "glasses," "spectacles."
- **un peu bourré:** is one of the expressions for "drunk," explained in Chapitre 6, page 73.
- **le mec:** "guy" ("bloke"). See also Chapitre 6, page 72.
- **le fute:** "pants," "trousers."
- **bof . . . Pas génial:** The expression **bof . . . !** with a shrug of the shoulders can mean a whole range of things, such as "So what?" "What can you do?" **Génial** is a useful adjective for expressing approval, like **super, chouette,** etc. See also Chapitre 4, page 46.
- **largué:** The verb **larguer** means to "cast off" a ship, so when **largué** is applied to a person it means that he is "not with it," "spaced out" ("all at sea").

AMER For Paul's girl (bird), who have we got? We need a chick who's got a lovely body, who's catchy, and a scream as well.

RICHARD Don't be such a worrywart. (Don't do your head in.) Stéphanie's a goer. I've already had a word with her about it.

- **Je-m'en-foutiste:** The expression **Je m'en fous*** is common for "I couldn't care less." ("I couldn't give a bugger.") From that expression, this adjective has been formed to mean someone who doesn't give a damn about anything.
- **du gâteau:** The expression **C'est du gâteau** means something is very easy, in fact, "It's a piece of cake."
- **mettre dans le coup:** means "to put (somebody) in the picture," and also, as here, "to win (somebody) over," "to convince (him)." The main meaning of the word **coup** is "a blow," but it is a useful all-purpose word in many expressions. For example, it might mean "a good blow" or "a rotten blow" dealt by fate, **un bon coup, un mauvais coup.** "To try your luck" is **tenter le coup** and if you succeed, you can use **réussir un beau coup.** If someone plays you a really dirty trick, it is **un sale coup** or **un coup de vache.** If you're going for a drink, you will **boire un coup** or **se payer un coup.**
- **la nana . . . une meuf:** both are words for "a girl," explained in the Language and Culture section in Chapitre 5, page 68.
- **bien foutue:** means "with a lovely body."
- **aguichante:** "enticing," "capable of attracting the guys."
- **marrant:** said of someone who is "good fun," "a laugh," "a bit of a scream." See also **se marrer** in Chapitre 5, page 62, and Chapitre 6, page 72.
- **Te prends plus la tête:** "Don't worry your head any more about it." Note other related expressions, such as **une prise de**

tête, "a real problem that's got to be solved." That could also be called **un casse-tête.** For someone who gets on your nerves, you can say **Il me tape sur les nerfs** or **Il me prend la tête.**

- **partante:** "ready and willing," "up for it."

VOCABULAIRE DU CHAPITRE

aguichante	enticing, attractive
une ambiance	atmosphere
un appart(ement)	apartment (flat)
un auteur	author
bien foutue	with a lovely body
les binocles	glasses, spectacles
Bonjour!	Hello! (See this chapter, page 98.)
le boucan	racket, row
la bouffe	meal, grub (nosh)
le bouquin	book
bourge(ois)	middle class
bourré	drunk
la casse-tête	difficult problem
Cassos.	Let's go.
castrer	to castrate
chiant*	boring
chier*	to shit
chier: On s'est fait chier.*	We were bored out of our minds.
la chierie*	something really tedious
le coup de vache	dirty trick
crade	filthy
cradingue	filthy
crado	filthy
crasseux	filthy
décontract(é)	relaxed, chilled-out, mellow

dégoter	to find
dégueu(lasse)*	disgusting
embaucher	to hire, to take a job
en chier*	to bust a gut
fourré	hanging out (holed up)
foutiste: je-m'en-foutiste	doesn't give a damn about anything
le fute	slacks, trousers
(c'est du) gâteau	(it's a piece of) cake
génial	terrific, great (brill)
glauque	sad place
la gueule	features, face
guindé	stiff, starchy, uptight
la hauteur	height
hyper-bondé	packed full
largué	not with it, spaced out (all at sea)
la librairie	bookshop
limoger	to fire (give the sack)
lourder	to kick out
lourder: se faire lourder	to be fired (to get the sack)
marrant	good fun, a bit of a laugh
le mec	guy (bloke)
mettre dans le coup	to convince, to win over
le mouchoir (de poche)	(pocket) handkerchief
partante	ready and willing, up for it
passer bien	to be well suited
rapidos	quick
réussir un beau coup	to succeed
le rigolard	joker
s'empiffrer	to stuff your face
se concocter	to concoct, to hatch (a plan)
se payer un coup	to go for a drink

se ramener	get together
tape-à-l'oeil	tacky
taper: Il me tape sur les nerfs.	He gets on my nerves.
Te prends plus la tête.	Don't worry yourself (your head) anymore about it.
tenter le coup	to try your luck
virer	to fire (give the sack)

À VOTRE TOUR!

A. Give the word or phrase that best fits each description. Choose from the following:

tape-à-l'oeil	**glauque**	**boucan**	**guindé**
mouchoir de poche	**dégueu**	**crade**	**hyper-bondé**

1. Il y a une ambiance formelle dans ce resto: c'est ___________.
2. Ça doit être sale à vous rendre malade: c'est carrément ___________.
3. Son appartement est tout petit: C'est grand comme un ___________.
4. Il se trouve dans un quartier peu sûr: c'est un quartier plutôt ___________.
5. Ce n'est pas très propre dans ce resto: c'est ___________.
6. La décoration n'est pas discrète et de mauvais goût: c'est ___________.
7. Il y a un bruit terrible dans cet endroit: Il y a un ___________ d'enfer.
8. Il y a toujours plein de monde ici. C'est ___________.

B. Give the word or phrase that best fits each description. Choose from the following:

aguichante	**rigolard**	**je-m'en-foutiste**	**marrant**
largué	**foutue**	**bourré**	**bourge**

1. Il a l'air un peu perdu: Il a toujours l'air ___________.
2. Il a l'air de se moquer de tout. Il est plutôt ___________.
3. Elle est très bien faite. Elle est bien ___________.

4. Il a souvent bu un coup de trop. Il est souvent ___________.
5. Elle est très attirante. Elle est ___________.
6. Ce mec là est très drôle. Il est ___________.
7. Il a toujours l'air de s'amuser. Il a l'air ___________.
8. Elle a une allure bon chic, bon genre. Elle a l'air assez ___________.

C. Complete the expressions on the left, and then match them to their English equivalent on the right.

1. Il avait _______ cet endroit moche.
2. Les clients ___________.
3. Qu'est-ce qu'on ___________ là!
4. Elle veut bien, elle est___________.
5. Ce soir, on ___________ tous chez lui.
6. C'est pas ___________ d'y arriver.
7. On doit ___________ un bon plan.
8. Elle a l'air assez ___________.

a. The customers are stuffing their faces.
b. He had dug up this terrible place.
c. It's not easy to get there.
d. We must cook up a good plan.
e. She's got a bit of a classy look about her.
f. We'll all get together at his place.
g. She has agreed to do it
h. Why were we hanging around (messing about at going) there?

D. Disagree using an expression with an opposite meaning.

1. — L'ambiance est très guindée dans ce restaurant.
   — Non! Je trouve au contraire que c'est plutôt ___________.
2. — Au resto des Arts, il y a un boucan d'enfer!
   — Non! C'est assez ___________ là-dedans.
3. — Il y a de la place dans l'appart de Guillaume.
   — Tu plaisantes? C'est ___________.
4. — Au moins, *Chez Alfred*, c'est assez propre, non?
   — Tu rigoles? C'est vraiment ___________ ce café-là!
5. — Claire dit que cette boîte a bonne réputation.
   — Non! C'est une boîte plutôt ___________.
6. — Admet qu'Éloïse ne cherche pas à attirer le regard!
   — Qui? Éloïse? Mais elle est très ___________ au contraire!

7. — Étienne, c'est ce mec là-bas qui est toujours intense?
   — Non, Étienne c'est un vrai ____________.
8. — Je trouve que Marie est trop vulgaire pour ce rôle, non?
   — Pas du tout! Elle fait au contraire très ____________.

HISTOIRES DRÔLES

— Alors, t'as trouvé un boulot?
— M'en parle pas! J'en avais décroché un à Limoges. Ils m'ont **limogé.** Ensuite, j'ai trouvé une place à Vires. Ils m'ont **viré.** Après, j'ai été embauché à Lourdes. Dix jours après, ils m'ont **lourdé.** Et hier, on m'a proposé un boulot à Castres. Je cours encore!

Just about impossible to translate! The verbs are all puns on the name of the French towns mentioned. **Limoger** and **virer** both mean "to give the sack"; **lourder** means "to kick out," and **castrer** means "to castrate." With this information, here is a lame translation of the joke:

"So, did you manage to find a job?"

"Don't even mention it. I got a job in Limoges and they sacked me (*limogé*). Then I got a job in Vire, and they sacked me (*viré*). Then I got a post in Lourdes, and they kicked me out (*lourdé*). Yesterday I was offered a job in Castres, and I haven't stopped running since."

★★★★★

Un Belge veut acheter un bouquin à la librairie de la gare avant de prendre son train.
— Madame la libraire, donnez-moi un livre, s'il vous plait.
— Quel **auteur** désirez-vous monsieur?
— Comment, quelle **hauteur**? Ça n'a pas d'importance pourvu que ça rentre dans le wagon!

A Belgian wants to buy a book at the station bookshop before catching his train.

"Excuse me, miss, I'd like a book please."

"Which author would you like, sir?"

"What do you mean, what height? It's of no importance as long as I can get it into the carriage!"

Another joke that is a play on words and so impossible to translate. The joke turns on the fact that the pronunciation of **quel auteur** and **quelle hauteur** are identical in French.

. Chapitre 9 .

J'avais craqué pour lui. Ça ne collait pas. Je l'ai plaqué.

Talking about the past • Remembering

Conversation 1

Éloïse fait ses confidences à Claire.

CLAIRE T'as l'air d'**avoir le blues.**

ÉLOÏSE Thomas vient de m'annoncer son mariage! J'y crois pas! On est sortis ensemble deux ans.

CLAIRE Oui, mais **ça fait un bail,** non?

ÉLOÏSE Oui, mais pour moi, c'est comme si c'était hier. C'était super. Il m'avait **dragué** dans **une boîte** et après il s'était **décarcassé** pour trouver mon adresse.

CLAIRE Oui, oui, et même que tu **râlais** parce qu'il **rappliquait** à toute heure, qu'il te **collait** tout le temps, qu'il te **pompait l'air,** que tu en avais **ras le bol.**

ÉLOÏSE Ça c'était au début. Après, j'avais **craqué** pour lui. Il se **mettait en quatre** pour me faire plaisir! Et puis, avoue, il

Éloïse has a heart-to-heart chat with Claire.

CLAIRE You look down in the dumps.

ÉLOÏSE Thomas has just told me he's getting married! I can't believe it! We went out together for two years.

CLAIRE Well, that was ages (yonks) ago.

ÉLOÏSE Yes, but it seems like just yesterday to me. It was brilliant. He hit on me (chatted me up) in a club, then he went out of his way to find my address.

CLAIRE Oh yeah, and you were moaning because he was popping up at all hours. He was latching onto you all the time, and he was bugging you. You'd had it up to the eyeballs.

ÉLOÏSE That was at the beginning. Then I really fell for him. He'd bend over backwards to please me. Besides, he was

	était joliement **baraqué**. Il faisait **de la muscu** trois fois par semaine.
CLAIRE	Ben justement à l'époque tu trouvais ça plutôt **nul**! T'arrêtais pas de lui **envoyer des vannes** parce qu'il était pas **intello**. Tu me disais qu'il était du genre tout dans les muscles rien dans la tête.
ÉLOÏSE	Vraiment, j'ai dit ça moi? Je ne m'en souviens plus!

ATTENTION AU LANGAGE FAMILIER!

- **avoir le blues:** "to be feeling down, low, depressed."
- **Ça fait un bail:** "It's been ages." ("It's yonks.")
- **draguer:** See Language and Culture, Chapitre 7, page 93.
- **boîte:** The basic meaning of **boîte** is "tin," "can," or "box," as in **des tomates en boîte** or **une boîte d'allumettes.** By extension, it can mean "a place where you work," such as an office. However, for many years it has been slang for "nightclub" (**boîte de nuit**) and now means "a place to go clubbing" (**aller en boîte**).
- **se décarcasser:** "to make every possible effort," "to bust one's back (a gut)," "to go to a hell of a lot of trouble." The origin of this expression is the word **la carcasse,** which means "the skeleton of an animal." By extension, it means "a human body." So **sauver sa carcasse** would be "to save your skin."
- **râler:** "to complain," "to nag."
- **rappliquer:** "to arrive," "to turn up."
- **Il te collait à toute heure:** "He stuck around you all the time." "He was always hanging around you." "He could never leave you alone."
- **Il te pompait l'air:** "He was bugging you." "He was getting you down." The literal translation of the French idiom is "He pumped out your air," meaning you couldn't even breathe on your own. This expression is linked to the use of **pomper** to mean "to exhaust," for example, **tout ce travail m'a pompé,** "all that work left me whacked/pooped."

built (hunky)! He worked out (did the gym) three times a week.

CLAIRE Well, that's just it. At the time you thought that was pretty sad. You were always giving him shit (jip) because he wasn't brainy. You used to say he was the type who had it all in his muscles and nothing in his head.

ÉLOÏSE Did I really say that? I can't remember that at all.

- **en avoir ras le bol:** means "to have as much as you can take," "to have a real bellyful." It can also appear as a noun, **le ras-le-bol,** meaning "the state of being totally fed up." You can see that the origin of this expression is a bowl that's full to the brim and ready to overflow.
- **craquer:** "to give way," "to weaken."
- **il se mettait en quatre:** He "cut himself into four pieces" to please her. So, we can say in English that he bent over backwards.
- **baraqué:** "muscular," "well-built."
- **de la muscu:** is short for **musculation,** meaning "exercises to develop muscles." Such abbreviations are encountered in Chapitre 8, for example **décontract, dégueu, appart,** and **bourge.** You might also like to note **p'tit déj (petit déjeuner)** and **la pub (publicité).** Later in this dialogue you will find **intello,** for **intellectuel.**
- **nul:** "worthless," "useless," "absolutely zero."
- **envoyer des vannes:** The meaning of **vannes** in this expression is "spiteful remarks," so you might translate this "to get at someone," "to say spiteful things." There is another, unconnected, meaning to the verb **vanner,** when it is used with the sense of "to wear out," "to exhaust." So, **Je suis vanné** means "I'm dead tired." This is another image that comes from farming. (See also **fauché comme les blés** in Chapitre 6, page 76.) The original meaning of **vanner** is "to winnow."

CONVERSATION 2

Julien et Aurélie se retrouvent à la rentrée. Ils se racontent leurs amours de vacances. Julien rentre de Grèce.

JULIEN Faut que je te raconte! Je suis sorti avec **une vraie bombe** suédoise. Une fille **carrément canon.** C'était galère pour la **draguer** parce qu'elle avait une copine qui lui **collait aux baskets** jour et nuit. C'était vraiment **délire!** On **s'est éclaté** ensemble, ça, on peut le dire!

AURÉLIE Et tu vas la revoir?

JULIEN On s'est téléphoné. Mais tu parles **c'est balèze!** On parle pas la même langue, alors il faut se parler en anglais et moi, je suis **une vraie bille** en anglais! Je vais être forcé **de faire une croix dessus.** Avec ces amours de vacances, il faut pas **se prendre la tête.** T'en profites **un max** et puis **tu te casses** et tu gardes tes souvenirs.

AURÉLIE Oui, t'as raison. Quand Juan s'est ramené à Paris, **j'étais sur le cul.** Dès son arrivée j'ai compris que **ça ne collait plus.** On avait rien en commun, il m'ennuyait. Ça a été **dur** mais **je l'ai plaqué.**

JULIEN En vacances, je veux passer du bon temps. **Une meuf** me plaît **je me la fais.** Point final.

ATTENTION AU LANGAGE FAMILIER!

- **une vraie bombe:** "a real bombshell!"
- **carrément canon:** You can say **c'est canon** to mean the same as **c'est super**, **c'est génial** (see also Chapitre 4, page 46), **c'est chouette**, **c'est géant**, and all the other ways of expressing total approval. In addition, **canon** can be used particularly for a really attractive girl, **une vraie bombe**. Add **carrément**, and Julien is really going over the top. You can add it to an adjective like this to reinforce it, and to mean there is absolutely no doubt about this.

Julien and Aurélie meet up at the start of term. They tell each other about their love life during the break. Julien is just back from Greece.

JULIEN I've just got to tell you this! I went out with some real Swedish babe (real Swedish talent). This girl was hot stuff (a hot bit of stuff)! It was tough hitting on her (chatting her up), because her friend trailed her day and night. But it was mad. We really had a wicked time together, I can tell you.

AURÉLIE Are you seeing her again?

JULIEN We've chatted on the phone. It's really, really difficult! We don't speak the same language, so we've got to speak English, and I'm a real loser in English. I'm going to have to call it a day. With these vacation (holiday) romances you mustn't get worked up about things (do your head in). Strike while the iron's hot, then split and keep your memories.

AURÉLIE You're right. When Juan came to Paris, I was flabbergasted. As soon as he turned up, it just didn't work any more. We had nothing in common, he bored me. It was hard, but I dumped him.

JULIEN On vacation (holiday), I want to have a good time. If I fancy a chick, I make sure I get her into bed. That's all there is to say.

- **qui lui collait aux baskets:** We've already had **coller** to mean "to stick to." In this case the friend is "sticking close to her heels," or, literally, "to her gym shoes (trainers)." You'll also find **baskets** in the expressions **Il est très bien dans ses baskets** (or **dans ses godasses**), meaning "He's at ease with himself."
- **délire:** another over-the-top word to express your sheer, total delight!
- **on s'est éclaté:** Juliette used this expression in Chapitre 7 to mean "We really hit it off together." (See Chapitre 7, page 87.)

RENCONTRE AVEC UNE FILLE CARRÉMENT CANON.

- **C'est balèze!** The original meaning of **balèze** is a "heavily built man." From that it comes to mean "great," "terrific." By a further extension it can be used ironically to mean quite the opposite, "tough" or "difficult." Here it is used with that touch of irony to mean they have a real problem, as they don't speak the same language.
- **une vraie bille:** You'll find the same word in **une bille de bois,** meaning "a block of wood." So Julien is useless at English.
- **de faire une croix dessus:** "to bring it to an end." In English one might say, "to draw a line under it."
- **Il faut pas se prendre la tête:** "You musn't get too worried about things."
- **T'en profites un max.** "You make the most of it."
- **Tu te casses:** "You leave." "Beat it." Note also the current use of **cassos**, meaning "Let's beat it." "Let's go."
- **J'étais sur le cul*:** These are more of those words that were once not often heard in conversation, but that occur in a number of expressions now. **Le cul** is basically what you sit on, whether

you call it "ass," "arse," or "bum." A number of related expressions mean "to be taken aback," "to be knocked over," for example, **être sur le cul★** and **rester sur le cul★.** Used as a noun or adjective on its own, it nearly always has something to do with sex, such as **Elle est très cul★** "She's really keen on it." There are a variety of other expressions, some quite entertaining, like **être comme cul et chemise★,** "to be thick with someone" ("to be as thick as thieves") (literally, "to be as close as ass (arse) and shirttail"). Of course, some expressions are particularly vulgar, for example, **Tu peux te le mettre au cul★,** "Go and stuff yourself." "Stick it up your ass (arse)."

- **Ça ne collait plus:** use of the verb **coller** once more, here meaning, "It just didn't work anymore" ("It didn't stick together any more").
- **Je l'ai plaqué:** means "I dumped him." See the discussion on the language of sex and love in the Language and Culture section in Chapitre 7, pages 93–95.
- **meuf:** is the verlan for **femme.** For an explanation of **verlan,** see the Language and Culture section in Chapitre 5, pages 67–69.
- **Je me la fais.** "I get her into bed." "I get laid." (See Chapitre 7, pages 93–95.)

VOCABULAIRE DU CHAPITRE

aller en boîte	to go clubbing
le bail	ages (yonks)
balèze: C'est balèze!	It's great! It's a real problem!
baraqué	built, hunky
les baskets	basketball shoes, gym shoes (trainers)
la bécane	computer, motorbike
la bille	block
le blues	depression, blues
la boîte d'allumettes	box of matches
la boîte de nuit	nightclub

la boîte	nightclub
la bombe	bombshell
canon	marvelous, terrific, the tops
carrément	absolutely, totally
la casquette	cap
le cédérom (CD-ROM)	CD-ROM
coller	to stick, to last
craquer	to give way, to weaken
la croix	cross
le cul*	ass (arse)
cul*: Elle est très cul.	She's really keen on it.
cul: être comme cul et chemise	to be thick with someone (to be as thick as thieves)
délire	marvelous, dreamy
des tomates en boîte	canned (tinned) tomatoes
la disquette	floppy disk
dur	difficult
en ligne	on-line
envoyer des vannes	to make spiteful remarks
faire: Je me la fais.	I get her into bed.
faire une croix dessus	to bring to an end
intello (= intellectuel)	intellectual
l'internaute	web surfer
l'internet	Internet
mailer	to E-mail
le max(imum)	maximum
la muscu(lation)	bodybuilding
nul	zero, worthless
plaquer	to dump, to drop
pomper (l'air)	to pump (air), to bug someone
râler	to moan, to complain, to nag
rappliquer	to keep coming around

ras le bol: en avoir ras le bol	fed up, as much as you can take
rester sur le cul*	to be taken back, knocked over
le routard	traveler, tramp
s'éclater	to hit it off really well
sauver sa carcasse	to save your skin
se casser	to leave, to beat it
se décarcasser	to bust one's back (a gut); to make every possible effort
se le mettre au cul*	to stick it up your ass (arse)
se mettre en quatre	to bend over backwards
se prendre la tête	to get worked up about things
le survêt(ement)	tracksuit
vanner	to wear out, to exhaust
le voyou	villain, criminal
le zonard	(seasonal) traveler

À VOTRE TOUR!

A. Match each word in bold with its definition.

1. **draguer**
2. **râler**
3. **rappliquer**
4. **plaquer**
5. **se décarcasser**
6. **craquer**
7. **se casser**

a. Être tout à fait séduit par quelqu'un ou quelque chose.
b. S'en aller, partir.
c. Terminer une relation avec un(e) petit(e) ami(e) qui n'a pas l'intention d'en finir.
d. Arriver, rejoindre quelqu'un, revenir dans un lieu.
e. Se plaindre de quelque chose, protester, grogner.
f. Aborder quelqu'un avec l'intention de la (le) convaincre d'avoir une aventure amoureuse.
g. Se débrouiller, faire vraiment tout ce qu'on peut pour arriver à quelque chose.

B. Unscramble the words to reveal the phrase that answers each question.

1. Et pour la draguer, c'était facile? ______________________

   Non! / galère / était / c'

2. Tu parles bien anglais? ______________________

   Moi?/ suis / bille / une / anglais / en / je

3. Avec qui es-tu sorti à Biarritz? ______________________

   Avec / bombe / une / suédoise / vraie

4. T'étais contente de le voir arriver? ______________________

   J' / cul / sur / étais / le

5. Et quel sport il faisait? ______________________

   muscu / de / fois / semaine / la / trois / par

6. Qu'est-ce qu'il faut faire
   après les vacances? ______________________

   casses / te / tu

7. Il y a longtemps que tu
   la connais? ______________________

   Oui, / bail / un / fait / ça

C. Complete the idioms in bold with the appropriate word or phrase from the chapter.

1. Je ne peux plus le supporter. Il est tout le temps derrière mon dos. **J'en ai** ________ de lui.
2. Marc fait les courses, la vaisselle, le nettoyage: il **se met** ________ pour lui faire plaisir.
3. Avec toutes ses histoires de mecs, elle commence franchement à **me** ________ **l'air.**
4. Elle a passé tout son temps hier soir à critiquer ce pauvre Marc et à **lui envoyer** ________.
5. Si tu vois Justine, c'est sûr que Marc n'est pas bien loin! Il **lui colle** tout le temps ________.
6. Notre histoire était trop compliquée: Elle habitait trop loin d'ici. J'ai dû **faire une** ________.
7. Moi, dans la vie je ne cherche pas les complications. Je ne **me** ______ pas **la** ________ avec des histoires qui n'en valent pas la peine.

D. What could you say in French in the following situations?

1. You feel a bit down.

   ____

2. You went out with a super sexy girl.

   ____

3. Explain that you picked her up in a club.

   ____

4. (S)he is calling you up at all hours.

   ____

5. You think (s)he is a pain in the neck.

   ____

6. You want someone to stop making cutting and hurtful remarks to you.

   ____

7. You have to give something up for lost.

   ____

LANGUAGE AND CULTURE

CHANGING SOCIETY, CHANGING LANGUAGE

We have already seen how the language is constantly changing to adapt itself to new forms of expression (Chapitre 5) and new social relationships (Chapitre 7). This section looks at more of those developments.

The information society In terms of the communication of information, France led the field with **Minitel,** which is still, for many people, a more important source of information than **le net,** also called **l'internet** or **le web.** An early attempt to use the French term **le réseau** seems to have been unsuccessful. Once you've got your **ordinateur** or, more colloquially,

bécane, perhaps you are **un accro du web** so you get **en ligne** whenever you can **pour surfer le net.** So you join the vast company of **internautes** seeking **les pages web** or **les sites web.**

As a member of the information society you will certainly have **une adresse e-mail.** There is still some doubt about a French version of E-mail, although the Academy, the guardian of the French language, has suggested a French form, **le mel.** It remains to be seen whether anyone will adopt this use, and the uncertainty is clear from a recent check on www.yahoo.fr. There, the search for **mel** gave access to a site offering **une adresse e-mail!** The verb **mailer** seems to have entered the language. Another site offers you information on **comment mailer vos amis.** Another English word that is used in this context is "saving" your E-mails in a file, which is **stocker dans un dossier.**

However, France actively tries to defend itself against the wave of English flowing in from the media. There are already some successes. **Le logiciel** is now normal for "software," a computer is definitely **un ordinateur,** and a floppy disk is **une disquette. CD-ROM** is now part of the language (pronounced, and sometimes spelt, **cédérom**). It is normal to refer to **une adresse e-mail** or **une adresse électronique.** When you write it for someone you might write **courrier él** followed by the address. When giving your address, you can refer to the sign @ either by its English name **at** or by the correct French term, **arobase.** If you want to get on-line, then Paris and other big towns already have their share of **cybercafés.**

Rap and techno terms Rap music has really taken off in France with performers like MC Solaar. This is not the place to discuss the differences between **le rap** and **la techno,** but they have had a significant effect on the language of young people, usually drawing heavily on English (West Indian) origins. Both have **des soirées raves** advertised on **des flyers.** Here is a section from an article describing the dancers: **on connaît le look des rappeurs—baskets, survêt, casquette portée à l'envers. Du côté des raveurs domine le piercing, qui consiste à se faire percer l'oreille, la narine, la lèvre. . . .** (We know what rappers look like—gym shoes [trainers], tracksuit, cap worn back to front. And the main thing to note about the ravers is body piercing, which means piercing an ear, a nostril, a lip. . . .)

Zonards** and **routards As soon as the fine weather comes, France starts to break out into a rash of festivals. And the people who visit these many festivals are, of course, **des festivaliers.** In addition to the festival-goers is a social group who don't actually go for the music or drama, but who hope to benefit from the crowd of well-off visitors as they sit on the pavement, often with a dog, and **font la manche,** in other words, they ask for small change from passersby. When one festival is finished, they move on to the next. These are **les zonards.** The word comes from the beginning of the twentieth century, when **la zone** was the popular term for the areas around Paris and other big cities that were run-down, shabby, and the haunt of tramps (**clochards**) and the out-of-work (**chômeurs**). So, the verb **zoner** came to mean "to be without a roof over one's head," and the down and outs were called **zonards.** The meaning of the word was extended as society developed and changed, so that it came to mean the deprived youngsters living in **la banlieue,** and was usually used with overtones of **voyou,** or criminal. Its location in the **banlieue** can be shown by the way the word developed a **verlan** form, **narzo.** Then, in its most recent mutation the word was applied to "travelers," the young people who choose to move around and live off the generosity of the passersby. There is a difference in the language between **zonard** and **routard.** The **zonard,** as we have seen, travels on a seasonal basis, when there are gains to be made, and in winter returns to **un squat.** The **routard** is always on the move. He is really a professional traveler or tramp.

Siglomanie French demonstrates great inventiveness in creating acronyms or **sigles** based on the words that form the title of the government measure. Such **sigles** and the words that derive from them form a significant part of the language of young people. So **SMIC** is **Salaire minimum de croissance,** the basic wage below which no employer may drop. Faced with an acronym, French will, of course, create new words, so someone on the basic wage is clearly **un smicard.** The **RMI (Revenu minimum d'insertion)** is unemployment pay that is paid to someone who is actively looking for a job. He or she is therefore **un(e) Rmiste.** Such formations are not unusual in French. For years, a member of the trade union **CGT** has been called **un CGTiste,** and Chapitre 7 gave an example of a very recent formation, the verb **pacser** following the passing of the **PACS** law in 1999.

Other common **sigles** are **SDF (sans domicile fixe)** for the homeless; **BCBG (bon chic bon genre)** meaning much the same as **bourge** and pronounced either **bécébégé** or **baisebeige.** In the more vulgar area is **SBAB** (pronounced **zbab**), which stands for **super bonne à baiser,** to describe a particularly attractive girl. There are some other common **sigles** used in this book: **CHU (cé-hâche-u)** for hospital (Chapitre 3) and **CDI (cé-dé-i)** for a contract with no fixed time limit (Chapitre 11).

. CHAPITRES DE RÉVISION 5–9 .

Review of Chapters 5–9

(50 points)

A. Solve the following crossword puzzle.

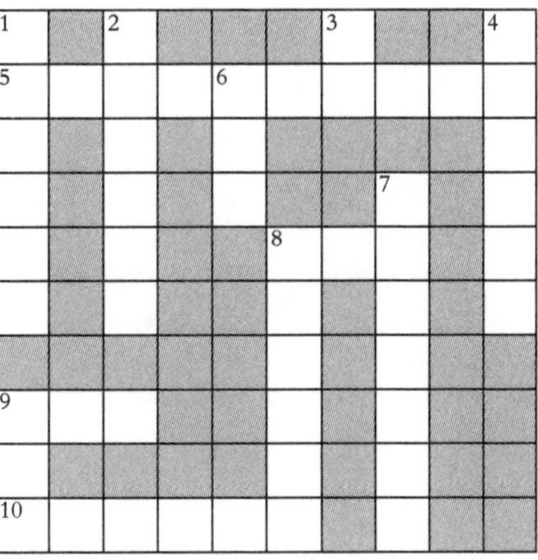

Horizontal

5. Fille qui aime attirer les garçons.
8. Tu t'asseois là-dessus!
9. Le maximum en raccourci.
10. Attacher; bien marcher (pour une relation amoureuse).

Vertical

1. Mot populaire pour parler d'une voiture.
2. Si on préfère être relaxe, on n'aime pas un restaurant _________.
3. Verbe aller à l'impératif.
4. Familier pour une moto ou un ordinateur.
6. Insulte signifiant "idiot", "crétin".
7. Avoir peur en langage familier.
8. Ne pas avoir du travail; ne pas perdre du temps.
9. Un type; un homme.

B. Match each French sentence to the correct English meaning.

13. Il a décidé d'aller en boîte.
14. Elle, c'était une fille canon.
15. Il l'a matée toute la soirée.
16. Elle s'éclatait avec ses copains.
17. Il est allé la baratiner.
18. Elle l'a trouvé assez marrant.
19. Il l'a trouvée craquante.
20. Il a essayé de la draguer.
21. Elle a commencé à en avoir ras le bol.
22. Il a continué à lui coller aux baskets
23. Elle a trouvé qu'il lui prenait la tête.
24. Il lui a filé un rencard.
25. Elle lui a posé un lapin.
26. Il s'est pris un râteau!

a. He found her really hot (dishy).
b. She began to be fed up with him.
c. He made a date with her.
d. He started to hit on her (chat her up).
e. He decided to go clubbing.
f. He was eyeing her up and down all evening.
g. She found him rather funny.
h. She and her friends were having a hell of a time.
i. He tried to pick her up.
j. He got dumped.
k. He kept on hanging around her.
l. She stood him up.
m. She felt he was driving her crazy.
n. She was hot stuff.

C. Find the right word or expression from the list to end each sentence:

une croix	**la crève**	**leurrer**	**flipper**
fringues	**piquer**	**pompes**	**lâcher**
accro	**bourré**		

27. Il veut nous faire croire que c'est pas sérieux avec Anne. Mais il la quitte pas. C'est clair qu'il est vraiment __________.
28. En sortant du bar, il tenait à peine debout et il racontait n'importe quoi. Il était complètement __________.
29. J'ai un entretien pour un job super demain. J'ai que des baskets à me mettre aux pieds. Il va falloir que j'aille m'acheter des __________.
30. J'ai un mal de crâne terrible et j'ai des frissons partout. Y faisait un froid mortel dans ce ciné. J'ai dû choper __________.
31. Tu croyais qu'elle avait gobé ton histoire? Et bien, plus la peine de te __________. Elle vient de me dire que t'étais un sale menteur!

32. Rentrer seul en pleine nuit et à pied dans ce quartier carrément glauque, j't'avoue que ça me fait __________.
33. Avec tout le boulot qui nous tombe dessus et deux collègues absents, les p'tites vacances à la neige, je vais devoir faire __________ dessus.
34. Il a cherché son porte-feuille partout. Il a fouillé sa bagnole, son appart'. Rien! C'est sûr qu'il se l'est fait __________ dans le métro.
35. Sophie vivait avec Cédric depuis sept ans. Mais quand elle a rencontré Fred, elle a pas hésité une minute à le __________.
36. J'adore faire les magasins. Je m'suis déjà payé ce mois-ci deux pantalons, une jupe et trois pulls! C'est dingue! Je vais me ruiner en __________.

D. Find the right French expression from the list below to fit each situation. Two expressions from the list will not be used. All these expressions have been used in Chapitres 5 to 9.

passer en coup de vent
être à l'ouest
ne pas en mener large
être à côté de la plaque
flasher sur quelqu'un
broyer du noir
se faire dépouiller
les bras m'en sont tombés
se faire des films

37. Simon had been drinking the whole evening. **Il** __________ **complètement** __________ **à la fin de la soirée.**
38. I had no news of you. I heard about this big accident on the train. I spent the whole evening on my own **à** __________.
39. It is quite dangerous to use this RER line after 11 P.M. There are a lot of muggings at night and often **on se** __________.
40. Paul had told me he would not stay because he was in a rush. I hardly talked to him. **Il** __________.
41. I was coming home at night and I noticed that three thugs were following me. I can tell you **j'**__________.
42. They had been going out together for years. When I saw her with Jacques last evening __________!
43. I will go to the interview tomorrow. Of course, it would be great to get this job. But I will see. **Je ne** __________.

E. Choose the correct meaning for the following French words or expressions.

44. You tell a friend how much you worry about the essay you haven't finished yet. He says **«Te prends pas la tête».**
    a. Don't worry!
    b. Good luck!
    c. Work harder.

45. You explain to someone the reasons why you cannot come to his party. He says to you **«Oui, encore des bobards!»**
    a. Yes, they are good reasons.
    b. I see. The same tales again!
    c. Well, I'll be very sorry.

46. You ask someone in a bar to give you a light. He stares at you without answering. Your friend says to you, "Don't worry." **«Il a un coup dans l'aile.»**
    a. He is very impolite.
    b. He is completely deaf.
    c. He's had too much to drink.

47. Fred asks Antoine if he could give him a lift to the airport. Antoine says, **«Faut pas charrier!»**
    a. That's pushing it. (It's a wind-up.)
    b. You've got a lot of nerve. (You are really cheeky.)
    c. It's a bit far!

48. You ask your friend how she has spent the weekend. She tells you she has just moved to a new apartment and adds **«J'ai pas chômé!»**
    a. I didn't hesitate.
    b. I didn't hang about.
    c. I did it on my own.

49. You are sitting on the terrace of a café with a friend. A guy is passing by. Your friend says to you **«Bien baraqué, le mec!»**
    a. He is a good-looking guy (chap)!
    b. He is real built (hunky)!
    c. He is so attractive!

50. You ask Emilie what the party was like yesterday. She had a great time until her boyfriend arrived but then she says **«Il m'a fait une scène».**
    a. He wanted us to leave.
    b. He made a scene. (He caused a stink.)
    c. He was in a dreadful mood.

. Chapitre 10 .

Ça te brancherait pas? Ça me semble un bon plan. On pourrait prendre ma caisse.

Making plans • Explaining your intentions

Conversation 1

Julien et Arnaud font des projets de voyage.

Julien **Y en a vraiment marre** de ce temps. Moi, j'ai envie de **me tirer** ailleurs, au soleil.

Arnaud Alors, là, je suis **partant.** J'irais bien faire une petite **virée** au Maroc. Ça te **brancherait** pas, toi?

Julien Oui, ça me semble **un bon plan.** Mais ce qui va être **galère** c'est de se trouver **une caisse** pour y aller. La tienne **tiendra** jamais **le coup** jusque là-bas! Tu t'es vraiment laissé **fourguer un clou!**

Arnaud Oui, ça, **y a pas photo!** On pourrait proposer à Guillaume de venir avec nous. Sa **bagnole** est plutôt chouette, non?

Julien Je lui **passe un coup de fil** ce soir. Si ça marche, on y va.

ON SE TIRE AU SOLEIL.

Julien and Arnaud make travel plans.

JULIEN I'm absolutely sick of this weather. I really feel like splitting. Somewhere else, in the sun.

ARNAUD Well, I'm game (two's up). I'd love to take a little trip to Morocco. How does that grab you?

JULIEN Yeah, that seems a good plan. But the real bummer is going to be finding a set of wheels to go there. Yours will never make it (take the blow till) there. You really were sold a real junker (a pup with that rustbucket).

ARNAUD That's the truth! We could suggest to Guillaume that he comes along. His wheels are in pretty good shape (nick), aren't they?

JULIEN I'll give him a buzz this evening. If it works out OK, we'll be off.

ARNAUD Si non, on pourrait y aller à **bécane!** Ce serait **kiffant,** non?

JULIEN Ouais, sauf qu'avec nos **meules d'enfer,** aller jusqu'au Maroc, **ça va craindre!** Ce qui est **con,** c'est qu'on pourra pas **se trimbaler** nos planches.

ARNAUD Je pense à une combine qui serait **top-délire.** Si Guillaume prend sa voiture, on lui **fourgue** les planches et nous, on descend à bécane! Génial, non?

JULIEN Là, tu **pousses** un peu! Il va penser qu'on le prend pour **un blaireau!**

ATTENTION AU LANGAGE FAMILIER!

- **Y en a vraiment marre de ce temps:** "I've had just about as much as I can take of this weather." See **avoir marre de** in Chapitre 2, page 20.
- **se tirer:** There is a whole range of verbs to express the idea of leaving; **se tirer** is one of the most common, together with **se sauver.** In the second conversation of this chapter you will find **s'arracher.** With more of a slang tone there is **se casser, se débiner,** or **foutre le camp*.** Also used for "to leave" or "to go out" is **se barrer,** for example, **Tout le monde se barre, y'a plus personne.**
- **partant:** "ready and willing," "up for it." See also Chapitre 8, page 104.
- **virée:** not a slang word, but a standard term for any sort of "trip," "drive," "spin."
- **Ça te brancherait pas?** The basic meaning of **brancher** is "to plug in," "to connect." From that you have the sense of **branché,** "switched on," and the use of the verb **brancher,** as used here, meaning "to turn on," "to grab," "to give a buzz."
- **un bon plan:** a good plan, but often used colloquially to mean the same as **une bonne idée.**

ARNAUD If not, we could go by motorbike. That would be awesome (pukka), wouldn't it?

JULIEN Well, yes. Except that with our old bikes, it'll be risky going all the way to Morocco. What's really stupid is that we won't (shan't) be able to drag our surfboards along with us.

ARNAUD I've just thought of a great scam that'll be so mad. If Guillaume takes his car, we ditch our boards with him and we go there by motorbike. Cool (mega), huh?

JULIEN You're pushing it a bit. He'll think we're taking him for a ride.

- **galère:** can be used as an adjective or noun to indicate difficulties. So you can say either **c'est la galère** or **c'est galère.** There is also a verb, **galérer,** meaning "to work really hard," for example, **avec la nouvelle organisation, il galère vachement.** The idea of **galère** meaning "really hard work" obviously goes back to the slaves in Roman galleys!
- **une caisse:** one of a number of colloquial words for "a car." Later in the conversation you'll also find **bagnole,** and other possibilities are **une tire, une chignole,** and, in Quebec, **un char.**
- **tiendra jamais le coup:** "will never make it," "will never last."
- **top-délire:** yet another way of saying "the very best," "the greatest." See also, **génial**, **super,** and **chouette** discussed in Chapitre 4, page 46.
- **fourguer:** means "to get rid of something by selling it to some unsuspecting person." Later in the dialogue it doesn't have the meaning of "to sell," but simply to load up the unsuspecting Guillaume with their surfboards.
- **Tu pousses un peu.** "You're pushing your luck."
- **un clou:** The first meaning of the word is "a nail," but it can be used to describe a broken-down wreck of a car (an old banger).

- **Y a pas photo!** "You're absolutely right!" The expression comes from horse racing, and the idea of a photo finish (for which the French is **une photo-finish**). Here, the idea is that Julien is so right that there's no need for a photo to prove it.
- **passer un coup de fil:** means "to telephone," "to call up," "to give someone a ring."
- **bécane:** Like the words for "car," there are a number of possibilities for "motorbike" ("mobylette"). **Bécane** is one of the most common, and nowadays, it is also a slang word for "a computer." Later in the dialogue is **meule,** with the same meaning. Another possibility is **une chiotte,** sometimes used for "an old car" but more common among the younger generation for "motorbike." (Note that this has nothing to do with the expression **C'est la chiotte,** "It's a really difficult job," or **aller aux chiottes★,** which is very vulgar for "to go to the lavatory.")
- **kiffant:** from the Arabic (see the Language and Culture section in Chapitre 5, pages 67–69) meaning the same as **chouette, super, hyper bien,** and so on.
- **Ça va craindre:** means "It'll be really difficult." See the note to **ça craint un max** in Chapitre 12, page 160.

CONVERSATION 2

Guillaume travaille depuis un an dans une boîte de marketing. Julien lui propose de venir avec lui et Richard faire une petite virée avec eux.

GUILLAUME Tu sais dernièrement je me suis complètement **investi** dans mon boulot. Je suis tellement **speedé. . . .**

JULIEN Ben, justement. Tu te **taperais** pas une petite pause en août? Ça te permettrait de **recharger tes batteries?**

GUILLAUME Tu sais, j'ai complètement **occulté** la question vacances jusqu'à maintenant. On doit **boucler** le nouveau projet pour la fin de la semaine—un boulot **d'enfer, j'te dis pas!** Je ne vais pas **émerger** avant lundi prochain.

ON POURRAIT PRENDRE MA CAISSE.

- **con:** Here, the word means "stupid," but see the more extended explanation in Chapitre 12, page 161.
- **trimbaler:** "to lug around," "to cart around."
- **un blaireau:** rather an insulting word, meaning "someone without importance but who thinks he is important." As a verb, **Je ne peux pas le blairer** means "I can't stand him."

Guillaume has been working for a year in a marketing firm (outfit). Julien suggests he might like to come with him and Arnaud for a little trip.

GUILLAUME Well, you see recently, I've been totally wrapped up in my work. I'm so stressed out.

JULIEN Well, that's just it. Why don't you treat yourself to a break in August? That would help you charge up your batteries.

GUILLAUME You know, I've avoided the idea of a vacation until now. (I'll tell you what. I've knocked the idea of holidays on the head.) We've got to wrap up the new project by the weekend—a real killer (stinker) of a job, I can tell you. I won't (shan't) be out of it till next Monday.

JULIEN Eh bien mardi, alors. On **s'arrache** mardi si tu préfères.

GUILLAUME Mais vous allez où au fait?

JULIEN Direction le sud, **c'est clair**. Après, **on improvise:** Maroc, Espagne, on verra en fonction **des thunes.**

GUILLAUME Et niveau transport, vous **assurez** comment?

JULIEN Ben là, y a encore rien de sûr. On pourrait prendre **ma caisse**, mais . . .

GUILLAUME Non, là, vieux, vraiment non. J'ai pas envie qu'on se retrouve à **l'hosto**. Je préfère prendre la mienne.

JULIEN D'accord! Alors, **c'est béton**? On se tire tous les trois mardi?

ATTENTION AU LANGAGE FAMILIER!

- **Je me suis investi:** "I've been completely wrapped up in my work." This is very much the language of the **jeune cadre dynamique** (dynamic young executive) whose work takes over him or her.
- **speedé:** When the word **speed** entered the French language at the end of the 1960s, it was borrowed from the drug culture, with the particular sense of amphetamines. So the adjective **speedé** had, at that time, only the sense of being under the influence of drugs. When the word spread more widely into colloquial language, it was given the same sense as **stressé.** The sense of **speedé** as far as drugs are concerned has been replaced by other words, for example, **camé, flippé, shooté, smaké.**
- **se taper:** here it means "treat yourself to." The expression is often used to refer to food and wine, for example, **On va se taper une bonne choucroute; On va se taper un bon p'tit vin.** It can sometimes have a rather negative sense, for example, **Je me tape toute la vaisselle,** "I've been stuck with washing the dishes."
- **recharger tes batteries:** as in English, means "to recharge one's batteries."

JULIEN OK, Tuesday then. We'll split on Tuesday, if you'd rather.

GUILLAUME Where are you going, anyway?

JULIEN Heading south for sure. Then we'll play it by ear. Morocco, Spain, it all depends on the cash (dosh).

GUILLAUME And as far as transport is concerned, how are you set up?

JULIEN Well, we could take my old junker (banger), but. . . .

GUILLAUME No thanks, my friend. I don't want us to end (land) up in the hospital. I'd rather take mine.

JULIEN Neat, so it's a deal. We'll take off, all three of us, next Tuesday.

- **occulter:** originally a highly technical word, used by astronomers to mean "to black out." It is used here colloquially to mean that Guillaume has completely shut the idea out of his mind. Like **s'investir,** noted earlier, this is another word from the vocabulary of the dynamic young executive.
- **boucler:** From its original meaning of "to fasten," "to tie up," **boucler** has come to mean also "to finish a job." **Boucler** is also used in the expression **la boucler** to mean "to shut your mouth," for example, **Vous allez la boucler, oui ou non?** "Are you going to shut your trap or not?"
- **un boulot d'enfer:** "a hell of a job."
- **J'te dis pas:** "You just can't imagine!"
- **émerger:** here means "to emerge," "to see the light of day," "to get the job finished."
- **on s'arrache:** See notes on **se tirer** from this chapter, page 132.
- **C'est clair.** "That's obvious."
- **on improvise:** "We'll make it up as we go along."

- **des thunes:** See the discussion on words for money in Chapitre 4, page 42.
- **vous assurez:** See the expression **j'assure un max** in Chapitre 3, page 31. It means "knowing exactly what has got to be done."
- **caisse:** See notes on **une caisse** from Conversation 1 in this chapter, page 133.
- **l'hosto:** an abbreviated form of **l'hôpital.**
- **béton:** From its original meaning "concrete," **béton** has come to mean "solid," "unshakable," "fixed."

VOCABULAIRE DU CHAPITRE

assurer	to know what's got to be done
la bagnole	car, automobile
la bécane	motorbike, computer
béton	fixed, solid
un blaireau	poor sap
boucler	to finish (a job)
le boulot	work, job
brancher	to appeal, to turn you on
la brique	brick, 10,000 francs
Ça va craindre.	It'll be difficult.
le cadre	executive
la caisse	car, automobile
camé	high (on drugs)
le char	car, automobile (**québécois**)
la chignole	car, automobile
la chiotte	motorbike (mobylette)
le clou	nail, old banger
le compte	bank account
con	stupid
émerger	to emerge, to get to the end of a job

flippé	high (on drugs)
fourguer	to sell, to hand over (to flog)
foutre le camp*	to leave, to beat it
galère	difficult (hard going)
l'hosto (= hôpital)	hospital
improviser	to make something up
J'te dis pas!	You just can't imagine!
kiffant	great, terrific
la meule	motorbike
occulter	to shut out completely
la paille	straw
paille: sur la paille	penniless
partant	ready and willing, up for it, keen
passer un coup de fil	to call, to phone
le plan	plan
plan: un bon plan	a good idea
pousser	to push, to exaggerate
recharger les batteries	to recharge one's batteries
s'arracher	to leave
s'investir	to devote oneself to or get wrapped up in (work)
se barrer	to leave, to go out
se casser	to leave, to beat it
se débiner	to leave
se sauver	to leave, to beat it
se taper	to treat oneself
se tirer	to leave
shooté	high (on drugs)
smaké	high (on drugs)
speedé	stressed out
stressé	stressed out
tenir le coup	to last
la tire	car, automobile

top-délire	fantastic, the tops
trimbaler	to lug around, to cart around
la virée	trip
Y a pas photo!	It's obvious! You're absolutely right!

À VOTRE TOUR!

A. Give a word or a phrase that best fits each description. Choose from the following:

tiendra pas le coup	**une virée**	**fourgué**	**galère**
se trimbaler	**occulté**	**y a pas photo**	**un blaireau**

1. J'ai accepté d'acheter une moto qui ne marche même pas! On m'a ________ un clou!
2. On va être obligé d'emmener tout un matériel. On va devoir ________ tout ça!
3. Ma voiture est trop vieille pour aller jusque là. Elle ne ________ jamais ________!
4. Elle ne voulait pas rester tout l'été à Paris. Elle avait envie de bouger, de faire ________ dans le sud.
5. Y a rien de plus difficile que de trouver un boulot ici. Ça va vraiment être ________ je te le dis!
6. J'ai essayé de ne plus penser à rien qu'à mon travail. J'ai donc complètement ________ la question loisirs.
7. Pauvre Guillaume! Julien et Arnaud lui font faire tout ce qu'ils veulent pas faire. Ils le prennent franchement pour un ________.
8. Avec le peu de travail qu'il fait il va encore râter son examen, ça ________.

B. Choose the response that best gives the real meaning of the following underlined idioms.

1. Ça serait <u>kiffant!</u>
    a. assez intéressant!
    b. super agréable!

2. C'est vraiment <u>con.</u>
   a. dommage.
   b. ridicule.

3. Ça me <u>brancherait</u> bien.
   a. ferait rêver.
   b. plairait et intéresserait.

4. On va <u>boucler</u> ça demain.
   a. terminer
   b. renvoyer

5. Pour ça, <u>il assure!</u>
   a. Il a la situation bien en main!
   b. Il se croit supérieur!

6. C'est <u>top-délire,</u> ce voyage.
   a. le plus amusant
   b. le mieux qu'on puisse avoir

7. <u>Ça va craindre!</u>
   a. Ne pas être très sûr!
   b. Ne pas être très comfortable!

8. <u>Y a pas photo!</u>
   a. Ça reste à prouver!
   b. C'est un fait sûr et certain!

C. Match the colloquial idioms on the left to their correct equivalent on the right.

1. Je vais me trouver un plan kiffant.
2. Je vais prendre ma caisse.
3. Je vais y aller avec ma meule.
4. Je vais lui fourguer ma bécane.
5. Je vais m'arracher.
6. Je vais trimbaler mon matos.
7. Je vais faire une virée là-bas.
8. Je vais recharger mes batteries.
9. Je vais me taper un boulot d'enfer.

a. Je vais me refaire des forces.
b. Je vais transporter le matériel.
c. Je vais devoir faire un travail énorme.
d. Je vais partir d'ici.
e. J'irai avec ma moto.
f. Je vais faire un petit voyage.
g. Je vais lui vendre ma moto.
h. J'irai en voiture.
i. Je vais faire un truc vraiment bien.

D. Unscramble the words to reveal the sentence that answers each question.

1. Qu'est-ce qu'on pourrait faire ce weekend?

   bien / virée / Belgique / en / faire / J'irai / petite / une

   ____

2. Pourquoi ne peux-tu pas venir avec nous?

   un / d'enfer / J'ai / boulot / actuellement

   ____

3. On ne te voit plus en ce moment. Qu'est-ce que tu fais?

   me / investi / mon / suis / Je / complètement / dans / travail

   ____

4. Quel serait le meilleur plan pour trimbaler nos planches?

   fourgue / les / planches / voiture / On / dans / la / Guillaume / de

   ____

5. Comment est-ce que t'aimerais y aller?

   y / On / aller / pourrait / bécane / à

   ____

HISTOIRES DRÔLES

— Ce cheval a déjà rapporté vingt **briques** à son propriétaire!
— Vingt briques! Et dire que malgré ça, cette pauvre bête mourra probablement **sur la paille!**

"This horse has already earned twenty bricks for his owner."

"Twenty bricks. And to think that the poor beast will probably drop dead on straw."

More plays on words! In French, **une brique** = 10,000 Francs. **Être sur la paille** means "to be penniless," and **mourir sur la paille** means "to die in poverty."

★★★★★

— Ainsi vous désirez m'épouser Gontran?—s'exclame Marie-Charlotte.— Mais vous ne me connaissez que depuis deux jours!
— Oh, ne croyez pas ça! Il y a dix ans que je travaille à la banque où votre père a son **compte.**

"So you want to marry me, Gontran?" cried Marie-Charlotte. "But you've only known me for two days!"

"Don't you believe it! For ten years I've been working at the bank where your father keeps his account."

You will remember the discussion about the use of **vous** and **tu** in the Language and Culture section in Chapitre 1, pages 10–13. So you will see that this couple must be rather aristocratic to still be calling each other **vous** when they are at the point of marrying!

. Chapitre 11 .

Ça te donne un look plus cool. Tu es drôlement bien sapé!

How to pay compliments and how to accept them
•
Gossiping

Conversation 1

Julien tombe par hasard sur Fabienne, une vieille amie qu'il n'a pas vue depuis un moment.

JULIEN — Fabienne! Salut! Dis donc, **ça fait un bail** qu'on s'est pas vus! **On se fait la bise.** Mais, dis donc toi alors, on peut dire que t'as l'air **en pleine forme!** Tu t'es fait couper les **tifs?** C'est vraiment super cette nouvelle coupe. Ça te va bien!

FABIENNE — Tu trouves? C'est sympa de me dire ça parce que j'étais pas trop sûre au départ, surtout de la couleur!

JULIEN — Mais non, ça te donne **un look** beaucoup plus **cool** qu'avant. C'est super je t'assure.

FABIENNE — Toi, on peut dire que tu es drôlement **bien sapé** ce matin: **costard-cravate, pompes** reluisantes. Tu fais **carrément** sérieux comme ça! Il faut dire que ça te va très bien le genre "jeune cadre dynamique".

Julien runs unexpectedly into Fabienne, an old friend he hasn't seen for a while.

JULIEN Fabienne! Hi! It's been ages (yonks). Give me a kiss. Hey, you really do look in (on) top form. Did you have a new hairdo? That new cut is cool (the biz). It really suits you.

FABIENNE D'you think so? It's nice of you to say so, because I wasn't really sure to begin with, especially the color.

JULIEN No, really, it gives you a style much more cool than before. Take my word for it, it looks really good.

FABIENNE Well, what about you? You're really dressed to kill this morning, I must say. Three-piece suit and buffed shoes (decks). You look dead serious like that. The "dynamic young executive" look certainly suits you.

JULIEN En fait je rentre juste d'un entretien d'embauche. **Tu m'aurais vu** il y a une heure. J'avais plutôt **les boules.** Et **figure-toi** qu'ils m'ont pris! Et en plus, c'est un **CDI!**

FABIENNE Non? Super! Félicitations! Je suis ravie pour toi . . . vraiment **ça s'arrose.** Je t'emmène **boire un coup.**

ATTENTION AU LANGAGE FAMILIER!

- **Ça fait un bail.** "It's been ages."
- **On se fait la bise:** A kiss on each cheek (sometimes three or four kisses altogether) is a usual greeting between friends.
- **en pleine forme:** "looking really good," "great," "the tops." Note the related phrases: **avoir la forme** "to be in great shape"; **tenir la forme** "to keep in shape," "to keep trim."
- **tifs:** colloquial for **les cheveux.** He's admiring her new hairdo.
- **un look:** an all-purpose word to describe your appearance, the way you dress, or the way you do your hair.
- **cool:** See Chapitre 7, page 85.
- **bien sapé:** The verb **se saper** means "to put your best clothes on," "to dress smarter than usual," so **bien sapé** is "very sharp."
- **costard-cravate:** A man's city suit is **un costard,** and **costard-cravate** is colloquially used to describe someone in formal wear. (The more formal French would be **costume-cravate.**) The ending **-ard** seems to be popular for forming slang words. Note also **connard*** meaning jerk ("twat, berk"); **ringard** meaning "corny," "old hat."

JULIEN Well, I've actually just had a job interview. You should have seen me an hour ago. I had the shakes. And get (cop) this, they hired me (took me on)! Even better, it's a permanent (fixed contract) job.

FABIENNE Really! That's terrific. Congratulations! I'm really happy for you. That's cause for celebration, I think (reckon). I'll take you somewhere for a drink (a bevy).

- **pompes:** are "shoes." See also the discussion on clothes (**fringues**) in Chapitre 6, page 76.
- **carrément:** "absolutely," "totally."
- **Tu m'aurais vu!** "You should have seen me!"
- **avoir les boules:** This means "to be really scared." If something is going to make you scared you can use **foutre les boules;** for example, **Moi, le tonnerre, ça me fout les boules.** Another meaning of **avoir les boules** is "to be angry," "to be fuming," but without showing anger.
- **figure-toi:** "Just imagine!" "Get this!"
- **CDI:** This is a **sigle,** like those mentioned in Chapitre 9, pages 123–124. This one means **un contrat à durée indéterminée,** that is, a contract with no fixed time limit.
- **Ça s'arrose:** "That deserves a drink!" **Arroser** is "to water" (the garden), so this phrase is used for any event that needs celebrating with some liquid.
- **boire un coup:** "have a drink." (See the notes on **coup** in Chapitre 8, page 103.)

CONVERSATION 2

Fabienne met Julien, qui a été absent cinq mois, au courant des derniers potins.

FABIENNE C'est **chouette** de te revoir! Au fait, t'es au courant pour Sophie et Guillaume, non? Faudrait pas que tu fasses de gaffe!

JULIEN Ben, non, je suis complètement **déphasé,** moi. Raconte.

FABIENNE Eh bien, ils ont **cassé.** Enfin, c'est plutôt elle qui l'a **plaqué.** Guillaume, il la voyait presque plus. Elle **s'éclatait** tellement dans son boulot qu'elle arrivait pas à **décrocher.** Il commençait à **en avoir sa claque.**

JULIEN Ils étaient encore ensemble à la fête d'Éloïse?

FABIENNE Oui, et c'est là que ça a **tourné au vinaigre.** Guillaume a passé la soirée à **tchatcher** avec une copine d'Éloïse qui, en plus, était **une** de ses **ex.** Sophie, ça **la gonflait pas mal.** Normal! Alors, elle a **piqué une crise.** **Elle lui a volé dans les plumes** devant tout le monde!

JULIEN Sans blague?

FABIENNE Pas étonnant, parce qu'elle **avait déjà un sacré coup dans l'aile,** mais lui, il avait tout fait pour la **faire sortir de ses gonds.** Elle l'insultait, elle **chialait.** C'était **mortel!**

Julien has been away for five months so Fabienne brings him up to date with the latest bits of gossip.

FABIENNE It's great to see you again. And are you up to date with the news about Sophie and Guillaume? You musn't go and put your foot in your mouth (in it).

JULIEN Well, no. I'm completely out of touch. Tell me all about it.

FABIENNE Well, they've split up. Well, to tell the truth it's really she who's dumped him (given him the elbow). Guillaume didn't get to see her much anymore. She was so wrapped up in her work she couldn't unwind. He was getting fed up with it.

JULIEN Were they still together for Éloïse's birthday party?

FABIENNE Yes, that's when everything turned sour. Guillaume spent the evening hitting on (chatting up) one of Éloïse's friends (mates), who was an old flame of his, to top it all. It was really pissing Sophie off (winding Sophie up). No wonder. So, she threw a fit (kicked up a fuss). She had a go (took a pop) at him in front of everybody.

JULIEN No kidding!

FABIENNE You might have expected it, 'cos she already had a drop too much to drink, but he'd done everything to make her hit the roof. She swore at him. She was crying (mental). It was awful (blubbering).

ATTENTION AU LANGAGE FAMILIER!

- **chouette:** See Chapitre 4, page 46.
- **déphasé:** means "out of touch."
- **casser:** means "to break" and here it's used with the sense of a couple splitting up.
- **plaquer:** "to dump" a partner; "to finish a relationship." (See Language and Culture section in Chapitre 7, pages 93–95).
- **s'éclater:** You've met this verb when it is used to mean "to get on really well together" (see Chapitre 7, page 87, and Chapitre 9, page 115). Here it means "to get a real buzz out of one's work," "to be totally committed to work."
- **décrocher:** means to "unhook," so here it has the sense of "switching off," "unwinding" after work. Compare the use of the opposite **accrocher,** meaning to "to be hooked," as when Juliette says **je suis plutôt accro** in Conversation 2 of Chapitre 7. When telephoning, **décrocher** is "to take the phone off the hook" and **raccrocher** is "to hang up."

- **en avoir sa claque:** "to have as much as you can take."
- **tourné au vinaigre:** "went sour."
- **tchatcher:** means "to talk a lot," "to chatter," and also "to hit on" ("to chat up"). So **la tchatche** can mean the same as **le baratin.**
- **une de ses ex:** "one of his ex-girlfriends," "an old flame."
- **Ça la gonflait:** "It got on her nerves." "It was pissing her off." ("It was winding her up.") The literal meaning of **gonfler** is "to inflate," as in **gonfler un pneu,** "to blow up a tire." Used colloquially it can mean anything from "to exasperate" to "to make you mad." If something really makes you mad, you can say **c'est gonflant.** The original phrase is **Ça me gonfle les couilles*** (literally, "That blows up/inflates my balls!"), and that is understood in the shorter form **Ça me les gonfle*** "It pisses me off." Compare this expression with **On se les gèle*** used to mean "We're absolutely freezing" in Chapitre 2, page 20. **Ça me gonfle les couilles*** is formed on the model of **Ça me casse les couilles*****,** "It really pisses me off." So a person or an event can be referred to as **casse-couilles*** ("ball-breaking" or "a real drag").
- **piqué une crise:** "threw a fit." Another expression with **piquer** is **piquer un fard,** meaning "to blush suddenly." On page 76, it is explained that **piquer** is also the slang verb for "to steal," as in **On m'a piqué mes fringues,** "Someone's ripped off (nicked) my clothes."
- **Elle lui a volé dans les plumes.** Literally, "She flew into his feathers," meaning "She really had a go at him."
- **Elle avait déjà un sacré coup dans l'aile.** Sticking to the bird metaphor, this is literally "She has already received a terrible blow to the wings," an expression that here means "She was drunk." "She had had a drop too much."
- **sortir de ses gonds:** The real meaning of this phrase is "to come off its hinges," talking about a door. When used for a person it means, "to fly off the handle," "to hit the roof."
- **chialer:** "to weep," "to shout" (see the Language and Culture section in Chapitre 7, pages 93–95).

- **mortel:** This word started off being used to describe something really bad, and then, as sometimes happens, came to mean the opposite, something really good! So it can have the same meaning as **super bien, fantastique,** or **génial.** Another example of such a reversal of meaning is the colloquial use of **terrible** to mean **formidable** or **super.** So, rather confusingly for a foreigner, **Ce film n'est pas terrible** means "This film is nothing special" or "It's nothing to write home about."

VOCABULAIRE DU CHAPITRE

accrocher	to get hooked on something
au fin fond	in the depths of
le baratin	chat
bien sapé	very sharp
la bise	kiss
boire un coup	to have a drink
boules: avoir les boules	to be scared
Ça fait un bail.	It's been ages.
Ça me les gonfle.*	It pisses me off.
Ça s'arrose!	That deserves a drink!
carrément	really, very
casser	to break up
CDI	contract with no fixed term
chialer	to shout, to scream, to weep
le connard*	jerk (twat, berk)
cool	cool
le costard	suit
costard-cravate	dressed formally
costume-cravate	dressed formally
cru	raw, uncooked
cuit	cooked
décrocher	to unwind, to relax, to take the phone off the hook

déphasé	out of synch, out of touch
en avoir sa claque	to have as much as you can take
en pleine forme	in (on) top form
faire sortir de ses gonds	to make somebody mad
gonfler	to exasperate, to annoy
un/une ex	ex-partner, old flame
le gaffeur	someone who keeps putting his foot in his mouth (in it)
un impair	blunder, gaffe
le look	appearance
minauder	to mince, to simper
mortel	marvelous
piquer une crise	to throw a fit
plaquer	to dump a partner
les pompes	shoes
prendre un coup dans l'aile	to have a shock
raccrocher	to hang up (phone)
ringard	corny, old-fashioned
s'éclater	to get a real kick out of something
s'égarer	to lose one's way
se figurer	to imagine
se saper	to dress smartly
tchatcher	to chatter
les tifs	hair
tourner au vinaigre	to turn sour
Tu m'aurais vu!	You should have seen me!
voler dans les plumes	to launch an attack

À VOTRE TOUR!

A. Choose the response that best gives the real meaning of the following idioms.

1. T'es drôlement **bien sapé.**
   a. bien en forme.
   b. bien habillé.

2. On se fait **la bise.**
   a. On s'embrasse.
   b. On se serre la main.

3. **Ça fait un bail** qu'on s'est pas vus.
   a. Il y a longtemps.
   b. Il y a un an.

4. Je suis complètement **déphasé.**
   a. Je ne suis plus au courant.
   b. Je suis plus accepté.

5. **Ça a tourné au vinaigre.**
   a. devenir une plaisanterie.
   b. devenir méchant.

6. Ça la **gonflait pas mal.**
   a. Mettre en colère.
   b. Faire grossir.

7. Elle lui a **volé dans les plumes.**
   a. se mettre en rage contre quelqu'un.
   b. critiquer les vêtements de quelqu'un.

B. Complete the expressions on the left and then match them to the English equivalent on the right.

1. Elle s'est fait couper __________.	a. He'd had as much as he could take.
2. Avant l'entretien, j'avais __________.	b. He is so wrapped up in his job.
3. C'est __________ de te revoir.	c. It suddenly went sour.

4. Tu __________ avant!
5. Il __________ vraiment dans son boulot.
6. Elle arrivait pas à __________.
7. Il en avait __________.
8. Ça a soudain __________.

d. She couldn't unwind.
e. It's great to see you again.
f. She had a haircut.
g. Before the interview, I was nervous.
h. You should have seen me before!

C. Connect the colloquial expression on the left with its more formal form on the right.

1. J'en avais ma claque.
2. Il a un sacré coup dans l'aile.
3. Il lui a volé dans les plumes.
4. Il l'a fait sortir de ses gonds.
5. Il est drôlement bien sapé.
6. Tu m'aurais vu.
7. Il l'a plaquée.
8. Il a un chouette costard.

a. Il s'est mis en rage contre lui.
b. J'aurais aimé que tu me vois.
c. Il porte des vêtements chics.
d. Il a un beau costume.
e. J'en avais assez.
f. Il lui a fait perdre patience.
g. Il a trop bu.
h. Il l'a quittée.

D. Make these compliments.

1. Tell her that her new haircut is great.

 ____

2. Tell her she really looks good.

 ____

3. Tell him that he is really dressed well this morning.

 ____

4. Tell him it is nice of him to say so.

 ____

5. Tell him he really looks very serious like that.

 ____

6. Congratulate him.

 ____

7. Tell her that it makes her look much more cool like that.

____

8. Tell him it's great to see him again.

____

HISTOIRES DRÔLES

Un complet **gaffeur** s'est bien juré de ne plus commettre **d'impair.** Arrivant chez des amis, il dit galamment à la maîtresse de la maison: «Chère Martine, comme vous avez changé!»

La dame **minaude,** «En mieux ou en pire?»

Et le gaffeur, sûr de lui cette fois, déclare: «Une femme comme vous, Martine, ne pouvait changer qu'en mieux!»

A man who couldn't help putting his foot in his mouth swore that he would never make such a blunder again. He arrived at the house of some friends and gallantly said to the lady of the house, "My dear Martine, how you have changed!"

The lady simpers, "Changed for the better or worse?"

And the blundering oaf, certain that this time he had got it right, said: "Ah Martine, a woman like you could only change for the better!"

★★★★★

Au siècle dernier, un missionnaire anglais s'est égaré dans un village tribal **au fin fond** de la campagne. Il s'est mis à prêcher l'évangile. Le matin, il n'était pas **cru.** Mais le soir . . . il était **cuit!**

In the last century an English missionary found himself in a tribal village deep in the country. He started preaching the gospel. In the morning they didn't believe him, but in the evening he was cooked!

There is no way of translating the play on words in French; **cru** = both "raw" and "believed."

. CHAPITRE 12 .

On a une grosse galère. C'est râpé. On aurait eu du fun!

TELLING SOMEONE HOW DISAPPOINTED/ HOW ENTHUSIASTIC YOU ARE

CONVERSATION 1

Marc annonce à Arnaud qu'il ne peut plus partir en vacances avec lui comme ils l'avaient prévu.

MARC Écoute, vieux. On a une grosse **galère.** Pour notre voyage en Espagne **c'est râpé.**

ARNAUD Attends là, **tu te fous de ma gueule** ou quoi?

MARC C'est **la tache** que t'as rencontrée. Il m'a annoncé ça avec un sourire de **faux-derche** du genre "Je t'emmerde je sais, mais t'as pas d'autre choix que de la fermer". Ils peuvent soi-disant pas me **lâcher** avant septembre. C'est fou, non?

ARNAUD Ah, **la vache.** J'y crois pas! **Ça craint un max.**

MARC Voir la gueule de ce sale petit con tous les matins! Crois-moi, **ça me sape le moral.**

Marc tells Arnaud that he won't be able to go on holiday with him as they had planned.

MARC Listen buddy (mate), we've got a huge problem (some grief). About our trip to Spain—it's off (down).

ARNAUD Just a minute. Are you kidding (taking the piss) or what?

MARC It's that jerk you met yesterday. He told me the news with that kind of two-faced smile that says, "I'm pissing you off, I know, but you've no other choice but to keep it shut." It seems that they can't ditch me until September. It's crazy isn't it?

ARNAUD That sucks! (What a pig!) I can't believe it! It's really the pits.

MARC Just think, I have to see that little shit's ugly face (stupid twat's ugly mug) every morning! It really gets me down! (It really drags you down!)

ARNAUD Moi, j'aurais **pété les plombs!** T'annoncer ça deux semaines avant, c'est vraiment **se foutre du monde!** Pas d'Espagne, **les boules,** alors!

MARC Écoute, tu ne vas pas **foutre** tes vacances **en l'air.** Ça serait trop **con.** Pars avec Éloïse.

ARNAUD **Tu délires!** Elle est **scotchée** à son ordinateur pour finir son mémoire. Non, laisse tomber. On va essayer de se refaire **un truc** en septembre.

ATTENTION AU LANGAGE FAMILIER!

- **une grosse galère:** "a real problem."
- **C'est râpé:** "It's all off!" You might also say **C'est fichu** or **C'est foutu,** or you can use the expression **C'est à l'eau** meaning "It's all off."
- **tache:** "jerk" ("berk," "twat") or any similar insulting term. (See Chapitre 1, page 7.)
- **faux-derche:** "two-faced," "hypocritical."
- **me lâcher:** "to let me go."
- **la vache:** "Shit!" "That sucks!" ("What a pig!") Other expressions would be **c'est vache** or **c'est galère.**
- **Ça craint un max.** The phrase **ça craint** can mean two quite different things, either "really bad" or "really great." Everything depends on the intonation! Here, clearly, it has a negative meaning.
- **Ça me sape le moral:** "That really gets me down." See also notes on use of **le moral** in Chapitre 5, page 58.
- **péter des plombs:** See Chapitre 2, page 21.

ARNAUD I would have blown my top. Telling you just a couple of weeks in advance! What a joke! (That's really taking the mickey.) No Spain. Bummer!

MARC Look, you musn't give up your vacation (holidays). That would just be too stupid. Go on vacation (holiday) with Éloïse.

ARNAUD You're crazy (mad)! She's glued to her computer to get her dissertation finished. No, forget it. We'll try again to get something planned (fixed up) in September.

- **se foutre du monde:** See a discussion of the use of **foutre** in Chapitre 2, page 16.
- **les boules:** an expression to indicate intense irritation, such as "I'm absolutely pissed off" (see Chapitre 11, page 147). It can also be used when you're really scared about something, for example, an interview; a bit like butterflies in the stomach.
- **con*:** The word has a double meaning. On the one hand it refers to the female sex organs, that is "cunt." On the other hand it means "stupid," and can be used either as a noun or adjective. So you can refer to someone by saying **Ce type est un con*** or **un petit con*,** or you can say **Tout ce qu'il dit est con*.** A feminine form has evolved so that you can insult a female, **Julia est encore plus conne* que Maria.** A slightly less insulting form is **connard*,** and a word that has lost most of its vulgar origins (though you should still use with care!) is **connerie*,** meaning a "stupid action" or "stupid statements." **Il n'arrête pas de dire des conneries*.** The verb **déconner*** (which is very vulgar!) means "to spout **conneries***"; for example, when telling someobody to shut up: **boucle-là! T'as assez déconné*.** So, as in English, this part of the female anatomy has come to be used for anything stupid. This is a sad state of affairs, as Georges Brassens, already mentioned in Chapitre 7, page 93, makes the

theme of one of his songs. He regrets that such a marvel of creation should have been given such vulgar usage in the language:

C'est la grande pitié de la langue française,
C'est son talon d'Achille et c'est son déshonneur,
De n'offrir que des mots entachés de bassesse
A cet incomparable instrument de bonheur.
(G. Brassens, *Le Blason*)

This might be loosely translated as:

It is the great sadness of the French tongue
Its Achilles' heel, a cause of dishonor,
That it offers only words that are stained with vulgarity
To name this incomparable instrument of joy.

- **Tu délires:** "You must be crazy!"
- **scotchée:** The trade name *Scotch*® for sticky tape has passed into the language as **le scotch.** So the verb **scotcher** means "stuck to," the same as **collée à.**
- **un truc:** "something or other." See also Chapitre 5, page 59.

CONVERSATION 2

Dialogue en québécois.

ERIC T'es pas venue hier à la réunion des anciens?

MARIE-ÈVE Hier soir j'étais complètement **brûlée** en rentrant **de la job.** J'ai pas eu le courage de ressortir.

ERIC **C'était plate** que tu ne sois pas là, tu sais. Henri a pris la parole, comme toujours. Il a **placoté** pendant trente minutes pour rien. Au bout de cinq minutes j'en avais **plein mon casque.** Il nous a même demandé de le payer pour la bouteille qu'il avait amené! Je te connais, **tu lui aurais fermé la gueule,** toi.

MARIE-ÈVE J'aurais **être en sacrement** je te le dis! Et j'aurais pas hésité à le traiter de **gratteux!** Philippe n'a pas réagi?

IL A PLACOTÉ PENDANT 20 MN.

A conversation between two French Canadians.

ERIC You didn't manage to come to the reunion last night?

MARIE-ÈVE I was burnt out when I got back from my job (earning a wedge). I couldn't face going out again.

ERIC Pity you couldn't make it. Henri dominated the conversation, as always. He was rambling (rabbitting) on about nothing for half an hour. After five minutes I had a real bellyfull. He even made us pay for the bottle he had brought. I know you would have shut him up.

MARIE-ÈVE I would have been fuming, I can tell you. And I wouldn't have hesitated to tell him what a jerk he is (what a mean sod he is). Philippe didn't react?

ERIC Il était pas là non plus! Avec lui au moins on aurait **eu du fun!** Mais il n'y avait que Jean et il est pas trop **jasant** lui, comme tu sais! Après ça, j'aurais aimé qu'on aille avec toute **la gang lâcher son fou** à la "Caverne". Mais, quand on est arrivé là, il y avait du monde **en masse.** On a jamais pu entrer!

MARIE-ÈVE J'ai bien fait d'aller me coucher!

ATTENTION AU LANGAGE FAMILIER!

Note that all the following words and expressions are taken from *québécois.* The equivalents from more standard French are also given.

- **brûlée:** "exhausted." In France you would say **crevé, claqué,** or **nase.**
- **la job:** "work." In France, **un job** usually refers to temporary work, that is, **un petit boulot.**
- **C'était plate:** means **C'était dommage,** "It was a pity."
- **placoter:** "to chatter away" in a rather superficial way; **bavarder.**
- **en avoir plein son casque:** "to have as much as you can stand"; **en avoir marre.**
- **Tu lui aurais fermé la gueule:** "You would have shut his trap." See the discussion on **gueule** in Chapitre 1, page 4.
- **être en sacrement (= être en colère):** "to be angry." Claude Duneton (see Bibliography) points out that *québécois* uses a number of religious expressions as swearwords, for example, **être en maudit; être en hostie; être en calvaire,** and so on. All have the same meaning as **être en sacrement.** The colloquial French equivalent is **être furax** "to be really mad."
- **gratteux:** This means "mean," "miserly," like the standard French **avare** and the colloquial **radin.**

ERIC	He wasn't there either. If he had been we'd have had a blast. But there was only Jean, and he's not chatty. In (at) the end I was hoping we would go with the whole gang and let our hair down at the "Caverne." But it was jam-packed. We never managed even to get in.
MARIE-ÈVE	I certainly made the right decision when I went to bed!

- **avoir du fun:** "to have fun," **s'amuser.** The expression **c'est pour le fun** has also become part of the language of young people in France.
- **jasant:** means "chatty," much the same as **bavard;** from the verb **jaser** "to chat" (= **bavarder**).
- **la gang:** "a group of friends"; **une bande d'amis.**
- **lâcher son fou:** "to have a ball," "to have a really great time." Compare **s'éclater, faire la bombe.**
- **en masse:** generally used to mean "plenty," for example, **de l'argent en masse** or **du monde en masse.**

VOCABULAIRE DU CHAPITRE

la balle	franc
béton	solid, firm
le bol	luck
les boules	bad luck
le bourge	yuppie
brûlé	tired
C'est à l'eau.	It's ruined. It's all off.
C'est fichu.	It's ruined. It's all off.
C'est foutu.	It's ruined. It's all off.

Ça craint un max.	That sucks. It's the pits.
Ça me sape le moral.	That really gets me down.
claqué	exhausted
coller à	to stick to
con*	stupid
le connard*	fool, idiot
les conneries*	stupid action, stupid statement
crevé	exhausted
déconner*	to talk absolute trash (rubbish)
délirer	to be crazy
en avoir marre	to have as much as you can take
en avoir plein son casque	to have as much as you can take
en calvaire, être	to be angry (*québécois*)
en hostie, être	to be angry (*québécois*)
en masse	plenty, masses
en maudit, être	to be angry (*québécois*)
en sacrement, être	to be furious
faire la bombe	to have fun, to have a ball
le faux-derche	hypocrite
fermer la gueule (à quelqu'un)	to shut somebody's mouth
foutre en l'air	to ruin completely
la francophonie	parts of the world where French is spoken
le fun	fun, pleasure
furax, être	to be really mad
la galère	difficulty
la gang	group of friends
gratteux	mean, miserly
jasant	chatty
la job	work
le joual	slang term for **québécois**

lâcher son fou	to have a great time
lâcher	to release
nase	exhausted
péter des plombs	to blow your top
placoter	to chatter
plate: (c'était) plate	(it was a) pity
radin	tight, miserly
râper	to fail
s'éclater	to have fun, to have a ball
scotcher	to stick
se foutre du monde	to make fun of someone (to take the mickey)
la tache	jerk (berk)
le truc	something or other
vache	rotten luck
La vache!	That sucks! (What a pig!)

À VOTRE TOUR!

A. Complete the expressions on the left, and then match them to the English equivalent on the right.

1. Pour notre repas au resto ce soir, c'est ________ malheureusement!
2. Ce type est ________, il faut s'en méfier.
3. Quand je vois tout ce boulot, ça me ________.
4. S'il recommence, je sais que cette fois, je vais ________.
5. A cause de lui, on a ________ nos vacances ________.

a. If he does it again, this time, I know I'll blow my top.
b. It's his fault that our vacation plans have been ruined.
c. About our meal in a restaurant tonight, it's off, I'm afraid!
d. This chap is a hypocrite; you must not trust him.
e. When I see all this work it drags me down.

B. Put a Q or an F after each statement to tell where it is used, in France or in Quebec.

1. Après deux jours de marche, j'étais vraiment brûlé. ____________________
2. C'est plate qu'il vienne pas ce soir. ____________________
3. J'en ai ras l'bol de le voir faire la gueule. ____________________
4. Il nous donnerait pas un sou, ce gratteux! ____________________
5. La job qu'il me propose est mal payée. ____________________
6. Il en a marre de faire ce boulot. ____________________
7. J'en ai plein mon casque de cette histoire. ____________________
8. Dans notre gang, c'est le moins jasant. ____________________
9. Perds pas tout ton temps à placoter. ____________________

C. Choose the correct French equivalent to the underlined *québécois* idioms.

1. J'étais en sacrement quand il m'a dit ça!
   a. fou de rage
   b. soulagé

2. J'ai besoin d'aller lâcher mon fou ce soir.
   a. rencontrer des amis
   b. aller m'éclater

3. Il a d'l'argent en masse.
   a. en quantité
   b. facilement

4. Sans lui, on aurait pu avoir du fun.
   a. bien se marrer
   b. bien boire

5. Il a réussi son concours? J'ai mon voyage!
   a. J'en reviens pas!
   b. J'avais raison!

6. Ces deux vendeuses placotent toute la journée.
   a. disent du mal des autres
   b. n'arrêtent de parler pour ne rien dire

7. Son cours de maths l'a complètement brûlé.
   a. crevé
   b. ennuyé

D. You meet a friend, and you've got things to tell him or her. What should you say in the following situations?

1. You are told a party you were looking forward to is canceled.

   ____

2. You want to tell a friend you've got a problem.

   ____

3. A friend tries to find a solution to your problem. You want to tell him to forget it.

   ____

4. You want to tell a friend that if that had happened to you, you would have blown your top.

   ____

5. You want to warn a friend that someone he trusts is in fact a two-faced person.

   ____

6. The date of a colleague's wedding falls in the middle of the month. That will completely ruin your vacation (holiday) plans.

   ____

7. You explain to your *québécois* friend that you are too tired to go to his party, although you know you would enjoy yourself there.

   ____

LANGUAGE AND CULTURE

THE VARIETIES OF FRENCH AND **LA FRANCOPHONIE**

The dialogues in this book have concentrated on the way the colloquial language is used in France. But there has been no space to give examples of regional French or of French as an international language. In this chapter we've given you a taste of the French of Quebec, so this is a good time to remember varieties of French found both within France and throughout the world.

The first characteristic to note in regional and international varieties of French is the variety of pronunciation. The French of the Midi or Quebec does not sound like the French of Paris. In the Midi, for example, the mute *e* at the end of many French words is sounded, making the language sound more like Italian or Spanish, for example, **une petite bouteille.** The Canadian pronunciation of **cheval** is **joual,** which has given its name to the language: **parler joual.**

Regional varieties are also characterized by local words or turns of phrase. For example, when counting in tens after sixty, the Belgians use **septante, octante,** and **nonante,** which do not exist in standard French. When asking you to repeat something, a French person may say **pardon?** or **comment?** But a Belgian will say **s'il vous plaît?** If a French person pushes past you, they will say **pardon** or **vous permettez?** But a Swiss will say **j'ose?** There are many such differences that you will note if you travel around different regions and countries where French is spoken. In North America, **québécois** is a major language, spoken by some 6.5 million people. Conversation 2 in this chapter has given you some examples of **québécois** expressions. These few examples cannot begin to explain the diversity of the French language, but they give a flavor of that variety.

The French-speaking world is called **la francophonie,** and people who speak French are **des francophones.** There are, of course, historical reasons for the spread of French, spoken in outposts of the former empire. Many of the countries speaking French have long been independent of French colonial rule, but a small number of territories are still classed under the heading **DOM-TOM (Départements d'outre-mer; Territoires d'outre-mer).** The inhabitants of these countries are French citizens with the right to elect representatives to the French parliament, and French is obviously the main language spoken and the language of administration.

Les DOM These are Martinique, Guyane, Guadeloupe, Réunion, St. Pierre et Miquelon.

Les TOM These are Nouvelle-Calédonie, Wallis et Futuna, Polynésie française, Mayotte.

Here is a summary of some statistics about the number of **francophones** in the world. (These figures exclude metropolitan France and the DOM-TOM.)

- **Maghreb and Middle East:** 16.2 million (particularly Algeria 7.5 m; Morocco 4.6 m; Tunisia 2.4 m).
- **Africa:** 15.2 million (particularly Côte d'Ivoire 3.6 m; Cameroon 2 m; République democratique du Congo 1.7 m).
- **Europe** (not counting France): 7.1 m (particularly Belgium 4.5 m; Switzerland 1.2 m; Romania 1 m).
- **North America:** 6.9 m (particularly Canada 6.6 m; USA [Louisiana] 0.3 m).
- **Caribbean:** 0.6 m (particularly Haiti).
- **Asia:** 0.1 m (particularly Vietnam; Vanuatu; Cambodia).

The extent of French language influence can also be judged from the worldwide range of newspapers in the language. There are, of course, many francophone newspapers in Canada, Belgium, Switzerland, and North Africa, but there are also papers in Togo, Bénin, Madagascar, Mauritius, Burundi, Lebanon, Burkina-Fasso, Gabon, and so on.

You may feel that you've got quite enough on your plate coming to terms with streetwise French, without having to bother about regionalisms and francophonie. A visit to a region or a country will bring you into contact with the particular local characteristics, and until then, it is enough to know that the variety exists and to marvel at the range and creativity of the language.

. CHAPITRE 13 .

C'est de la daube! J'en avais ma claque! C'est franchement délire!

SAYING WHAT YOU LIKE AND DON'T LIKE

•

EXPRESSING YOUR VIEWS AND YOUR PREFERENCES

•

SAYING THAT YOU AGREE OR DISAGREE

CONVERSATION 1

Armelle et Stéphane sortent du cinéma. Ils entrent dans un café pour discuter du film.

ARMELLE C'est **de la daube** ce film. L'histoire est **nase,** les acteurs sont **minables.** C'est vraiment **foutre son fric par la fenêtre** d'aller voir un pareil **navet!**

STÉPHANE Alors, là, **j'hallucine!** Comment tu peux dire des **conneries** pareilles? C'est franchement **délire** ce film. Le moment dans le métro quand les deux **loubards** s'engueulent, c'était mortel! Et ce type complètement largué. Sur ce **coup-là** il a vraiment assuré.

Armelle and Stéphane are leaving the cinema. They go into a café to discuss the film.

ARMELLE That film really was the pits. The story is lame (zero); the actors are pathetic. It's like throwing your money down the drain to go and see such a turkey.

STÉPHANE Unreal! How can you talk such trash (rubbish)? That film is awesome (wicked). That moment in the metro when the two thugs were arguing (giving each other grief), that was really deadly. And then the guy who was completely spaced out—the director was really right on (spot on) at that point.

ARMELLE Eh bien moi, j'y ai rien **capté** de cette histoire. En plus, il n'y a pas d'action. Au bout d'une heure, j'en avais **ma claque. C'est nul.** Tu verras que ça va être **un bide** complet! Je te le dis!

STÉPHANE **Tu veux rigoler.** Je viens d'entendre qu'il a déjà fait le plus grand nombre d'entrées de la semaine.

ATTENTION AU LANGAGE FAMILIER!

- **de la daube:** "rubbish," "useless." The expression is often used to describe poor quality electrical equipment, for example, **C'est de la daube, ta chaîne hi-fi,** "Your hi-fi unit is absolute crap."
- **nase:** This word has a number of meanings. Here, referring to the story of the film it could be translated "feeble." When referring to a person it means "exhausted." It can also refer to a piece of equipment that is broken and unusable, for example, **Ma bagnole est nase.**
- **minable:** "hopeless," "useless," "pathetic."
- **foutre son fric par la fenêtre:** Here is the all-purpose **foutre** yet again, this time meaning "to throw your cash out of the window," or as we might say in English, "down the drain."
- **navet:** actually a "turnip," but used to refer to a play or film in the same way as "turkey."
- **conneries:** "trash," "rubbish." (See discussion of the family of words related to **con** in Chapitre 12, pages 161–162.)
- **J'hallucine:** "I can't believe what I'm hearing."
- **délire:** "great," "terrific," "brilliant."
- **loubards:** "thugs," "hooligans."
- **sur ce coup-là:** the reference here is to a film "take." So that particular take was "something else!" The director really knew what he was doing (**Il a vraiment assuré**).

ARMELLE Well, I just couldn't make heads or tails of the story. And besides, there's no action. After an hour I'd had a bellyful. It's absolute crap. You'll see, it'll be a total flop. I tell you.

STÉPHANE Now you really are joking. I've just heard that it's already had the biggest audiences of the week.

- **J'y ai rien capté:** "I just didn't get it at all." In telecommunications, **capter un message** means "to pick up a message." In colloquial speech it means "to understand," or, when used in the negative, "can't make heads or tails of."
- **J'en avais ma claque:** "I'd had as much as I could take." Compare this expression with **J'en avais marre** and **J'en avais ras le bol** discussed in Chapitre 2, pages 17 and 20 and Chapitre 9, page 113.

(See Conversation 2.)

- **C'est nul:** "It's absolutely zero, crap, useless."
- **un bide complet:** "a total failure." The word **bide** is used for any sort of show in the theatre or cinema (**un bide retentissant,** "a resounding failure") and, by extension, in any other field. If you come up with a new project that gets the

CONVERSATION 2

Claire et Fabien sortent d'un repas chez leurs voisins qui les ont invités à diner.

CLAIRE T'as pas trouvé que Patrick n'avait pas l'air de **tenir la forme?** On aurait dit qu'ils **étaient en froid** tous les deux.

FABIEN Oui, oui. T'as vu **la tronche qu'il tirait** quand Annette racontait son voyage à New York? Il a pas **desserré les dents** de tout le repas!

CLAIRE Faut dire qu'elle **abusait** un peu, non? J'ai trouvé ça **un peu gros** quand elle insistait sur ce type **super sympa** assis dans l'avion à côté d'elle. **Faut pas pousser! C'était vraiment vache** pour lui qui était resté **bosser** à Paris.

FABIEN Oui. Mais le **bouquet** c'est quand ils ont commencé à **s'engueuler** dans la cuisine!

CLAIRE J'ai vraiment l'impression que leur couple ne va pas **faire long feu.** En tout cas, c'est clair qu'il **y a de l'eau dans le gaz** entre eux. **Pas de bol!** Le réveillon chez eux, c'était plutôt délirant, non? **C'est grillé** pour l'an prochain.

thumbs-down, you can say, **Alors mon nouveau projet, c'est le bide complet.**

- **Tu veux rigoler:** "You've got to be joking." **Rigoler** is a very common verb to use instead of **rire,** "to laugh." See also notes on **rigoler** and **se marrer** in Chapitre 5, page 62.

Claire and Fabien have just left friends who had invited them to dinner.

CLAIRE Did you find that Patrick didn't seem to be himself this evening? You'd think that the two of them were at odds with one another.

FABIEN Yes, you're right. Did you see the face he made (was pulling) when Annette was telling the story of her trip to New York? He was on edge (screwed up) all through the meal!

CLAIRE Still, you must admit that she went a bit too far, don't you think? I thought it was a bit over-the-top to keep on about the really awesome (mega) guy sitting next to her on the plane. There is a limit! It was a bitch for him, considering he stayed in Paris to work.

FABIEN Yes, but the final straw for me was when they started to duke it out (to have a slanging match) in the kitchen.

CLAIRE I have a feeling their relationship will fizzle out shortly. Anyway, it's clear that there's a storm brewing between them. We're unlucky. New Year's Eve at their place was quite a laugh, wasn't it? That's blown it for next year!

ATTENTION AU LANGAGE FAMILIER!

- **N'avait pas l'air de tenir la forme:** means "He was not quite himself." "He was not behaving as you might expect."
- **être en froid:** "to be on very bad/icy terms."
- **la tronche qu'il tirait:** "the face he was making (pulling)." The use of **tronche** is discussed in Chapitre 1, page 4.
- **desserrer les dents:** "To grit or clench your teeth" is **serrer les dents.** So in this case, Patrick's teeth stayed gritted or clenched all evening!
- **abuser:** "to push things too far," "to overdo it."
- **un peu gros:** "a bit over-the-top."
- **super sympa:** "absolutely awesome (mega)!" This is the most unbelievably nice guy you could possibly meet!
- **Faut pas pousser:** "You shouldn't push your luck."
- **C'était vraiment vache:** "It was really the pits." See also Chapitre 5, page 59.
- **bosser:** means "to work hard."
- **le bouquet:** normally a "bunch of flowers," of course, but it can also be used to mean "the climax or crowning piece in a firework display." From that, **C'est le bouquet** means "the last straw," ("that takes the biscuit")! A more formal way to say this in French is **C'est un comble.**
- **s'engueuler:** means "to yell at each other." See the Language and Culture section in Chapitre 7, pages 93–95. The root of the word is **gueule,** which has appeared in a number of preceding chapters.
- **faire long feu:** This expression is often used, as here, to mean "to last for some time." But more exactly it means "to be a letdown" ("to be a damp squib"), that is, something that was supposed to be quite an event but that never really made it. This is from the origin of the expression, when a gun was primed to

shoot but the gunpowder was wet, so the weapon **fait long feu,** meaning "It didn't go off properly."

- **Il y a de l'eau dans le gaz:** literally, "There's water in the gas," so it means that "Things are not running too smoothly."
- **Pas de bol.** "Out of luck." (See Chapitre 1, page 6.)
- **c'est grillé:** like steaks that have stayed on the grill too long, plans for next New Year are "burned to a crisp (cinder)," "ruined."

VOCABULAIRE DU CHAPITRE

claque: en avoir sa claque	to have as much as you can take
abuser	to exaggerate
baladeuses: (des mains) baladeuses	wandering (hands)
becter	to eat, to chow (to nosh)
le bide	failure
bosser	to work hard
le bouquet	bunch of flowers, high point
broncher	to move a muscle
capter	to understand, to grasp the meaning
les conneries	trash, rubbish (balls)
la daube	trash, rubbish
délire	great, marvelous
desserrer les dents	to unclench one's teeth
eau: Il y a de l'eau dans le gaz	Things are not running smoothly.
faire du pied	to play footsie
faire long feu	to last, to be a letdown
Faut pas pousser.	Don't push your luck.

filer	to slip (money)
forme: tenir la forme	to be in good shape
foutre par la fenêtre*	to throw out of the window, to throw down the drain
grillé	ruined
gros: un peu gros	over-the-top
halluciner	to fantasize
minable	pathetic
nase	feeble
le navet	turnip, turkey (failed play/film)
outré	outraged
pas de bol	out of luck
peloter	to fondle (to touch up)
rigoler	to laugh, to joke
s'engueuler	to shout at each other
SDF (= sans domicile fixe)	homeless person
sympa (= sympathique)	nice, super, cool (mega)
tirer une tronche	to make a face (to pull a face)
la tronche	face

À VOTRE TOUR!

A. Match the ends of the expressions on the right with the correct beginning on the left.

1. J'en ai	a. dans le gaz.
2. Ils ont l'air d'être	b. capté.
3. Faut pas	c. tronches!
4. Il y a de l'eau	d. ma claque.
5. C'est foutre son fric	e. les dents.
6. J'ai pas desserré	f. en froid.
7. Elle tirait une de ces	g. pousser.
8. J'y ai rien	h. en l'air.

B. Disagree, using an expression with an opposite meaning. There is more than one possible answer in each case.

1. — Quel beau film!
   — Moi, je trouve que c'est ______________.
2. — Ça va être un succès total.
   — Tu parles! Ça va être ______________.
3. — Les acteurs étaient vraiment excellents.
   — Tu rigoles? Ils étaient ______________.
4. — Avec ce film, j'ai pas vu le temps passer.
   — Et bien moi, après cinq minutes, ______________.
5. — J'ai trouvé ce livre génial.
   — Pour moi, il est tout à fait ______________.
6. — Julien avait l'air en pleine forme.
   — Mais non! Il ______________.
7. — Entre eux deux, ça va durer, tu verras.
   — Et bien moi, j'te dis que leur couple ______________.
8. — J'ai bavardé un bon moment avec lui.
   — Bizarre. Avec moi, il ______________.

C. Imagine that you are talking with your friend's father or mother. Replace the underlined colloquial word or expression with one or two more formal and more polite synonyms from the following list.

gâcher mon argent	**fichu**	**nul**	**se disputer**
dur	**je rêve**	**faire la tête**	**assez**
excitant	**des bêtises**		

1. Pour moi, ce film, c'est <u>de la daube.</u> ______________________________
2. Ce genre de pièce au bout de dix minutes, j'en ai <u>ma claque.</u> ______________________________
3. Notre sortie? C'est <u>grillé</u> pour ce soir. Alex a la grippe. ______________________________
4. Hier avec Julien, <u>on s'est engueulé</u> toute la soirée. ______________________________
5. Je peux pas supporter quand il commence à <u>tirer la tronche</u> comme ça. ______________________________

6. J'ai l'impression d'avoir <u>foutu mon fric en l'air!</u> ________________

7. Il flirte avec Anne sous son nez. C'est <u>vache</u> pour elle. ________________

8. Un film comme ça, <u>c'est délirant!</u> ________________

9. Alors là, <u>j'hallucine!</u> ________________

10. Arrête de dire des <u>conneries</u> pareilles. ________________

D. What would you say to a friend of your own age in the following situations?

1. Tell him you've spent the whole day arguing with Anne.

   ____

2. Warn him that buying this CD is throwing money down the drain.

   ____

3. Ask him if he agrees that the party yesterday was a flop.

   ____

4. Tell him the film you've just seen is absolutely great.

   ____

5. Ask him why he was on edge (screwed up) all through the party.

   ____

6. Tell him this novel is the pits and you could not make heads or tails of the story.

   ____

7. Tell him to stop talking trash (balls).

   ____

8. Tell him he's got to be joking when he says that this play is such a turkey.

   ____

HISTOIRES DRÔLES

Au cinéma un type âgé s'installe avec sa jeune femme. Le voisin de la jeune femme commence à lui **faire du pied** et a les **mains très baladeuses.** Le mari ne bronche pas. Une **nana** assise derrière est **outrée.** Elle tape sur l'épaule du mari et lui dit: «Monsieur, vous feriez bien de regarder ce qui se passe à côté de vous. Le type à droite de votre femme est en train de la **peloter** outrageusement!»

«Je sais», répond le vieux. «Quand je vais au cinéma c'est toujours comme ça. Mais si je la laisse à la maison, on me la **baise**. . . . »

In the movie theatre, an old fogey came and sat down with his young wife. The guy next to the wife started to play footsie and let his hands wander. The husband didn't move. A chick sitting behind them got really mad. She tapped the husband's shoulder and said, "You ought to take a look at what's going on next door. You should see how the guy in the seat next to your wife is feeling (touching) her up."

"I know," said the old wrinkly. "It always happens when I go to the pictures. But if I leave her at home she gets fucked."

★★★★★

Un **SDF** s'adresse à un jeune **bourge** pressé.

«Zavez pas cent **balles?** J'ai rien **becté** aujourd'hui.»

«Vous êtes pas le seul, moi non plus!»

«Dans ce cas» réplique l'autre, «**filez**-moi cinq cent balles. J'vous inviterai au **resto.**»

A homeless dropout tried to beg from a young yuppie in a hurry.

"Got any change? I've had nothing to eat all day."

"You're not the only one! Nor have I."

"If that's the case," answered the dropout, "slip me a few bucks (quid) and I'll take you out to dinner."

. CHAPITRE 14 .

Ça s'arrose à mort! À la tienne! À la nôtre!

ORDERING IN A RESTAURANT • PROPOSING A TOAST

CONVERSATION 1

Julien annonce à Guillaume qu'il vient d'obtenir le travail qu'il voulait.

GUILLAUME Ça, **ça s'arrose à mort!** Allez, on **se prend** d'abord un p'tit **apéro** pour **se mettre en train.** Pour moi, ce sera un scotch bien **tassé.** Qu'est-ce que tu prends?

JULIEN Moi, une **mousse** peut-être . . . non, **un p'tit jaune** pour une fois.

GUILLAUME À la tienne! À la nôtre! Au boulot qui t'attend! Et félicitations!

*(Il avale son verre **d'une traite.**)*

JULIEN Dis-donc, t'as une **sacrée descente,** toi! Tu peux en **écluser** combien comme ça?

GUILLAUME Ça y est! Dis tout de suite que tu me prends pour un **pochtron!** Me **défoncer** à l'alcool c'est pas mon truc, mais dans certaines

Julien tells Guillaume that he has just landed the job he wanted.

GUILLAUME Well that's worth partying for! Come on, we'll start with a little drink just to get in the flow of things. I'll have a large scotch. What are you having? (What's yours?)

JULIEN Perhaps a beer? No, just for once I'll have a pastis.

GUILLAUME Cheers! Here's to both of us! And here's to the work that's waiting for you. Congratulations!

(He downs his drink.)

JULIEN Wow! You can knock it back! How many can you down (sink) like that?

GUILLAUME Hey, watch out. Why not say straight out (straight away) that you think I'm a drunk (piss artist)? Well, getting wasted on

occases, je **crache** pas sur une bonne petite **picole,** c'est tout. Allez, on **remet** ça? On **s'en jette** un dernier?

JULIEN Juste un alors, parce que moi, avec les apéros, **j'assure** pas. Au troisième j'suis **rétamé grave.**

ATTENTION AU LANGAGE FAMILIER!

- **Ça s'arrose à mort:** "That's really worth celebrating!" You could also say, **Ça s'arrose à fond.**
- **On se prend:** "Let's just grab a quick . . ." In colloquial French there is a tendency to use a reflexive verb in these situations: **On se prend un p'tit apéro; On s'envoie un p'tit canon; On se fait une petite bouffe.** The reflexive gives the idea of "treating yourselves," "doing yourselves a favor." The colloquial tone is increased by the use of **petit** (even if you intend to have a large one!).
- **un apéro (= apéritif):** English does not use the term *aperitif* as frequently as French. We'd be more likely to say "a drink."
- **se mettre en train:** means "to go (get) with the flow," "to get in the mood." More formal French might say, **se mettre dans l'ambiance.**
- **mousse:** "beer."
- **un p'tit jaune:** means **un pastis** or a Pernod.
- **boire d'une traite:** "to down (sink) your drink in one gulp (go)."
- **T'as une sacrée descente:** "You can certainly knock it back!"
- **écluser:** means "to down" ("to sink") a drink (or a lot of drinks!). **Une écluse** refers to the locks on a canal that fill up with water!
- **un pochtron:** "a drunkard" ("a piss-artist").
- **(se) défoncer:** to "get wasted" on alcohol (or drugs).
- **occase:** another abbreviated form, this time for **occasion.**

booze is not my thing, but, for the right occasion I don't knock a little drinking (piss-up). Same again? One more for the road?

JULIEN Well, just one then. The trouble is, when it comes to spirits, I can't hack it. By the time I get to the third I'm well hammered.

- **cracher (sur quelque chose):** means literally "to spit on" and therefore, "I've got nothing against."
- **une picole:** "booze," together with the related verb **picoler.**
- **s'en jeter un:** see the notes in the Language and Culture section of this chapter for a selection of words meaning "to have a drink."
- **Remettre ça:** "Have another one."
- **(être) rétamé:** "to be hammered"; see the selection of words for "drunk" in Chapitre 6, page 73.
- **grave:** See the note to **saturer grave** in Chapitre 2, page 17. The adjective **grave** is used instead of the adverb you would expect here, so it means "I'm seriously hammered/drunk."

(**On se connaît?** Do we know each other?)

CONVERSATION 2

Julien, Guillaume, et Éloïse célèbrent l'anniversaire d'Armelle dans un petit ***resto*** *de quartier.*

GUILLAUME D'abord, pas de **pinard** aujourd'hui. On va **se payer** un bon petit Bordeaux pour l'occasion. Ils en ont un, vous m'en direz des nouvelles! J'en sais quelque chose, j'ai **une ardoise** ici.

JULIEN Alors, voyons la carte. Moi, je me **taperai** bien une petite queue de langouste, ce soir, pas vous? C'est toi qui **régales,** Armelle, non?

ÉLOÏSE Pour elle, c'est **cadeau.** Mais toi, tu vas nous **coûter la peau des fesses,** avec ta langouste! Alors on commande? J'ai rien **becté** depuis ce matin. Je commence à **avoir les crocs.**

JULIEN Ouais, alors **magnez-vous,** parce qu'Éloïse, elle est **pas de bon poil** quand elle a **l'estomac dans les talons.** Moi aussi d'ailleurs **j'ai la dalle.** J'espère que le **cuistot n'y regarde pas** sur la quantité. Je **crève de faim.**

ÉLOÏSE Bon, je résume: du canard, du homard, des escargots. . . . J'te vois déjà en train de **te creuser les méninges** Guillaume. Ton petit discours, je le sens, on va pas y **couper!** Bon, alors, **on trinque** d'abord à Armelle. **À la tienne** et bon anniversaire!

ATTENTION AU LANGAGE FAMILIER!

- **pinard:** This is **vin** that is very **ordinaire,** so "cheap wine" ("plonk").
- **se payer:** See the notes following Conversation 1 in this chapter for the use of the reflexive verb in these circumstances.
- **(avoir une) ardoise:** "to have a tab (slate)." See the notes in the Language and Culture section of this chapter.

Julien, Guillaume, and Éloïse celebrate Armelle's birthday in a little local restaurant.

GUILLAUME Well now, first things first, no cheap wine (plonk) today. We'll treat ourselves to a really nice bottle of Bordeaux for the occasion. They've got one here. You can tell me what you think about it. I've got a tab (slate) here.

JULIEN Come on. Let's have a look at the menu. I could murder a little lobster tail this evening. How about you? Armelle, it's your treat (shout) isn't it?

ÉLOÏSE Well, it's our treat to her, but you're going to cost us an arm and a leg with your lobster. Shall we order? I haven't eaten since this morning. I'm beginning to feel famished.

JULIEN Come on, we'd better get a move on. Éloïse gets a bit testy (shirty) when she's got a hole in her stomach to fill. Come to think of it, I'm hungry too. I hope the chef isn't skimpy with the portions. I'm starving.

ÉLOÏSE Right, I'll sum it up. There's duck, lobster, snails—but I can see you're already deep in thought, Guillaume. I feel we're not going to be able to get out of hearing your little speech. OK, let's drink to Armelle first of all. Here's to you, and happy birthday (many happy returns).

- **se taper:** widely used with the sense of "to eat with pleasure." Here it is **une queue de langouste,** but you might very well say **Je me taperai bien une bonne choucroute** or **On va se taper la cloche,** "We're going to have a superb meal."
- **régaler:** means "to treat" somebody to a meal or a drink.
- **C'est cadeau:** "It's a treat." **C'est cadeau (= je te l'offre).** You could also just say **cadeau!** or **gratos.** But note that the expression is *not* **C'est un cadeau.**

- **coûter la peau des fesses:** This means literally that it will "cost you the skin off your ass (arse)." A rather more vulgar form of the same expression is **coûter la peau du cul*.** The equivalent English is a bit less expressive: "to cost an arm and a leg."
- **becter:** is an alternative to **bouffer** for "to chow," "to eat" ("to nosh").
- **avoir les crocs:** "to be very hungry." A more common expression with the same meaning is found later in the conversation, **Je crève de faim.** You've also got **Elle a l'estomac dans les talons,** meaning, literally, "Her stomach is in her heels," and also **avoir la dalle.** Using the same word, **casser la dalle** means the same as **casser la croûte,** "to have a meal."
- **se magner:** a slang word for "to get a move on." Another possibility would be **se grouiller.**
- **être de bon/mauvais poil:** "to be in a good/bad mood." The origin of this idiom lies in the word **poil,** meaning "hair." You might imagine that stroking hair in the right direction would put somebody into a good mood, and that's the reason for **être de mauvais poil.** This word occurs in a number of useful idioms. In Chapitre 2, it was said that the line (queue) **n'avance pas d'un poil,** meaning "not even a very tiny bit." Also useful is the idiom **à poil** "naked" and **se mettre à poil** "to strip off." After an illness you can **reprendre du poil de la bête,** meaning "to regain strength," "to recover." This has much the same sort of image as the English "hair of the dog that bit you."
- **cuistot:** This is colloquial for "the chef" of a restaurant.
- **ne pas y regarder:** means, here, that he hopes the cook is generous when it comes to the quantities he serves up. The expression is used whenever you mean that someone doesn't care how much something costs, "to not pay any attention to expense."
- **se creuser les méninges:** "to rack one's brains."
- **On ne va pas y couper:** "We won't (shan't) be able to get out of it."
- **trinquer:** "to clink glasses," "to drink a toast."

- **À la tienne/À la vôtre:** is what you say as you raise your glass, meaning **À ta santé** or **À votre santé.**

Vocabulaire du chapitre

À la tienne/À la vôtre!	Cheers!
une andouille	fool (sort of sausage)
un apéro (= apéritif)	drink, aperitif
ardoise: avoir une ardoise	to have a tab (slate)
arroser	to celebrate with a drink
becter	to eat (to nosh)
la bouffe	meal, something to eat
bouffer	to eat, to have a meal
Ça s'arrose!	That deserves a drink!
cadeau: C'est cadeau.	It's a treat.
le canon	drink
cloche: se taper la cloche	to have a good meal
couper (ne pas y couper)	to cut (not to miss)
coûter (la peau des fesses*)	to cost (an arm and a leg)
cracher (sur quelque chose)	to say no to, to spit on
crever (de faim)	to die (of hunger)
crocs: avoir les crocs	to be famished
croûte: casser la croûte	to have a meal, snack
la cuisine	cooking
la cuisine du terroir	regional cooking
le cuistot	chef
dalle: avoir la dalle	to be hungry
descente: avoir une descente	to knock it back
écluser	to knock back (to sink) (your drink)
estomac: avoir l'estomac dans les talons	to be very hungry

les fruits de mer	seafood
le gigot	leg of lamb
grave	serious(ly)
jaune: un p'tit jaune	pastis
jeter: s'en jeter un*	to down a drink
magner/se magner	to get a move on
la mousse	beer
une occase (= occasion)	occasion
la picole	boozing
le pinard	cheap wine (plonk)
le pochtron	drunkard (piss artist)
poil: être de bon/mauvais poil	to be in a good/bad mood
poil: n'avancer pas d'un poil	to advance hardly at all
poil: reprendre du poil de la bête	to recover (from a hangover)
le poivrot	drunkard
régaler	to treat someone else
regarder: ne pas y regarder	to be generous
remettre	to have another
le resto (= restaurant)	restaurant
rétamé, être	to be hammered (legless)
se creuser les méninges	to rack your brains
se défoncer	to get wasted
se grouiller	to get a move on
se mettre en train	to get with the flow
se payer	to treat yourself
se prendre (un apéro)	to have a drink
se taper	to treat yourself
le soûlard	drunkard
tassé: bien tassé	a good measure

train: se mettre en train	to get in the flow
traite: boire d'une traite	(to drink) in one swallow
trinquer	to clink glasses, to propose a toast to someone
les viennoiseries	pastries

À VOTRE TOUR!

A. Match the slang expressions on the left to their correct equivalent on the right.

1. J'avais les crocs.
2. Leur cuistot est minable.
3. Ce resto coûte la peau des fesses.
4. Il a une sacrée descente.
5. Je crevais de faim.
6. Il a éclusé toute la soirée.
7. On arrose ça ce soir?
8. Il s'est tapé deux entrées.

a. On va fêter ça en prenant un verre?
b. Il a pas arrêté de boire de la soirée.
c. Je mourrais de faim.
d. Il a pris et mangé deux entrées.
e. Ils ont un mauvais cuisinier.
f. C'est un restaurant très cher.
g. Il boit beaucoup et facilement.
h. J'avais très faim.

B. Replace the underlined expressions with their slang equivalent from the list below:

avoir la dalle	**se magner**	**pochtron**	**être rétamé**
becter	**cracher sur**	**avoir une ardoise**	**mousse**

1. Il est dix heures. On a un train dans cinq minutes. Écoute, <u>dépêche-toi!</u> On va le louper. ______________________

2. On a pas arrêté toute la journée. Même pas une minute pour manger. <u>J'ai vraiment faim.</u> On rentre dans ce petit resto? ______________________

3. C'est mon bistrot ici. J'habite à cent mètres. Le patron me connaît bien. D'ailleurs <u>j'ai un compte</u> ici. ______________________

4. Incroyable! Quel trou ce bled! Ça fait dix minutes qu'on cherche, mais on trouve rien à <u>manger</u> ici: pas un seul resto! ______________________

5. Dix heures de rando en pleine montagne et sous la chaleur. Je donnerais tout pour me taper une petite bière bien fraîche! ____________

6. Ce type passe sa vie dans les bars. Tu vas pas me dire qu'il est pas devenu un alcoolique! ____________

7. On a fêté l'anniversaire de Pierre hier. Comme j'étais crevé ce soir-là, au troisième verre, je ne tenais plus debout. ____________

8. Armelle a toujours l'air très sérieuse, mais j'peux t' dire que quand elle sort, elle ne dit pas non pour l'apéro. ____________

C. You are in a café with a group of friends, celebrating Julien's new job. Do the following:

1. Tell them you must drink to this occasion.

   ____

2. Suggest to start with an aperitif.

   ____

3. Say you must all drink to Julien.

   ____

4. Say "cheers" to Julien.

   ____

5. Congratulate him.

   ____

6. Drink to his job.

   ____

D. In which situation should you use the following phrases? Write the letter **I** for a very informal situation and the letter **F** for a more formal situation. Write the formal equivalent for each informal phrase, and vice versa.

1. J'aime pas l'eau. J' bois que du pinard. ______

   ____

2. Il me semble qu'il est plutôt éméché. ______

____

3. Ça va nous coûter une fortune! ______

____

4. On va se payer une bonne bouffe. ______

____

5. Allez, on s'en jette encore un! ______

____

6. C'est dingue ce que j'ai les crocs. ______

____

7. Il picole et après, il est de mauvais poil! ______

____

8. Lui, on voit vite qu'il boit pas mal! ______

____

LANGUAGE AND CULTURE

EATING AND DRINKING

Celebrating a piece of good news with a drink (**ça s'arrose!**) is a French habit of very long standing. One might just have **un apéro** (**un apéritif**), possibly **un p'tit jaune** (**un pastis** or **un pernod**), or whisky has become quite popular, so **un scotch** will fill the bill. There is a whole range of expressions for "to have a drink," for example, **boire un coup, prendre un pot, s'en jeter un, s'envoyer un verre.** If it's beer (which has grown in popularity), it can be **boire un demi, prendre une blonde** or **une brune, boire une mousse,** or **une pression** (draught beer). If it's wine, you can **boire un canon, prendre un coup de blanc, s'envoyer un coup de rouge, se payer un bon petit pinard.** If you go down to your local **bistro** for your **apéro** you might drink standing at the bar, **le zinc.** If you are a regular customer, you might even put it on the tab (slate) (**une ardoise**). Contrary to what you might think, the traditional **bistro** is not a place to eat, but simply for friends to gather and have a drink. Of course, there is the downside to drinking alcohol, and in Chapitre 6, page 73, you were given a selection of the words for "drunk." Someone who makes a habit of drinking a lot (**picoler**) is **un pochtron, un poivrot,** or **un soûlard.** Perhaps it is these associations that have given the **bistro** a rather negative connotation, in contrast to **le café,** which is much more acceptable to a wider section of society.

With the changing habits of drinking and eating, it is estimated that 200,000 traditional **bistros,** which existed in 1960, have been reduced to fewer than 50,000. Although alcohol remains associated with **la fête, le plaisir, et la convivialité,** there have been significant changes in drinking habits over the years. The consumption of alcohol has dropped recently. In 1950 the average intake of wine, for example, was 126 liters per person per year. This had dropped to 60 liters in 1997. (This still leaves the French among the biggest consumers in the world.)

As far as food is concerned, that is clearly a very high priority on any French list of the things that matter in life. Finding **un bon petit resto** is an important achievement, and, at the top end of the market, the status of restaurants and their chefs is unmatched anywhere else. When the Michelin guide awards stars for food, it is on the basis that one star—**vaut la visite;** two stars—**vaut un détour;** but three stars—**vaut le voyage!** For a meal to be worth a journey (and possibly a long journey) shows that this is an important aspect of the culture, not just feeding your face. When a three-star chef leaves, it makes front-page news in the national press and the restaurant loses the stars until it can demonstrate that it has appointed someone who can guarantee the same quality. At the other end of the scale, another guide to eating out just divides its recommendations into **vite fait; bien fait; bonne bouffe; resto de fête.** The colloquial words for *eating* are **bouffer** or **becter,** or you can say, as in the conversations of this chapter, **je me taperai bien . . .** meaning, "I would really like to eat. . . ." There are a variety of words for having a meal, for example, **casser la croûte, casser la graine, se faire une bonne bouffe.**

Eating out continues to grow as a national leisure pursuit. The national expenditure on eating out has doubled from 10 percent of the food budget in 1965 to 20 percent in the late 1990s. There has been considerable growth by commercial restaurant chains such as **Hippopotamus** and by fast-food outlets (**le fast food**). There is now more snacking, and a good deal of the money spent on food is now spent in **sandwicheries** (26 percent), **viande-grills** (11 percent), and **pizzerias** (10 percent). It is some consolation for lovers of tradition that the French still eat far more sandwiches than hamburgers, but within the younger generation, things are changing. Among fifteen- to nineteen-year-olds, the order of preference is **steak-frites,** followed by **couscous** and then **le hamburger** in third place. (The order of preference for those over sixty is **le pot-au-feu, le gigot,** and **la blanquette!**) Twenty-one percent of the younger age-group drink Coca-Cola with their **déjeuner** and "graze" on cakes and **viennoiseries** ("pastries") between meals. (**Grignoter** is "to nibble" or "to graze.") It could be that the national passion for gastronomy is changing. One commentator poses the key question: **La tradition gastronomique française survivra-t-elle à l'uniformisation des habitudes alimentaires?** ("Will the French gastronomic tradition survive the growing uniformity in eating habits?" G. Mermet in *Francoscopie: Comment vivent les Français,* Larousse, 1999. This publication is also the source of statistics in this section.)

A more comforting thought is that the French government takes the issue of food very seriously and has introduced sessions for developing tasting skills into school programs (**la semaine du goût**). Also encouraging is the fact that regional cooking traditions (**la cuisine régionale; la cuisine du terroir**) still seem to be cherished. You can still expect superb seafood (**les fruits de mer**) in coastal regions, **crêpes** in Brittany, marvelous local cheeses in Normandy and in mountain regions, **choucroute** in Alsace, **cassoulet** in the Languedoc, **bouillabaisse** in Marseilles. The French colonial heritage also offers the pleasures of North African (**couscous** and **tajine**) and Vietnamese cooking. Despite all the cultural changes and international uniformity, France remains one of the places where you can be sure of eating well, and usually, of being served by people who not only know about food, but have had first-rate training in a catering school, or **école hôtellière.**

Histoire drôle

Un client appelle le serveur:
— Et bien, garçon, mon **andouille** n'arrive pas vite!
— Je ne pouvais pas savoir que monsieur attendait quelqu'un!

A customer calls over the waiter:
"Waiter, my sausage hasn't arrived yet."
"I didn't realize that you were waiting for someone, sir."

Une andouille is a sort of sausage, but the word also means a "dum-dum," "a stupid fool."

. Chapitres de révision 10–14 .

Review of Chapters 10–14

(50 points)

A. Solve the following crossword puzzle.

Horizontal

1. Sens premier: voir des choses qui n'existent pas. Sens actuel: Verbe utilisé pour traduire un grand étonnement devant un fait auquel on ne peut croire.
4. Mot familier pour désigner l'argent.
6. Mot familier pour désigner une moto.
8. Verbe significant "se débarrasser de quelque chose ou de quelqu'un".
11. Sens premier: protéger contre un danger. Sens actuel: être maître de la situation—savoir ce qu'on fait.

Vertical

2. Mot argotique pour désigner des choses stupides, des bêtises.
3. Bateau dans lequel les Romains utilisaient des esclaves pour ramer; mot très utilisé actuellement signifiant «dur, pénible, difficile».
4. «Fête» en verlan.
5. Sens familier: fêter un événement heureux en buvant ensemble.
7. Mot familier pour «les cheveux».
9. Partie d'une porte qui permet d'ouvrir et fermer. Ce mot, utilisé avec le verbe «sortir» signifie «exploser de colère».
10. Mot qui, utilisé dans le sens familier, signifie «une voiture, une moto qui ne marche pas bien, qui est une mauvaise affaire».

B. Qu'est-ce que je peux dire à mon copain? Match each description to the correct English meaning.

13. Tu es un mec super sympa.
14. Tu as un look très cool.
15. T'es toujours bien sapé.
16. Tu t'es fait couper les tifs.
17. Tu t'investis à fond dans ton boulot.
18. T'as besoin de recharger tes batteries.
19. Tu n'arrives pas à décrocher.
20. Tu sors vite de tes gonds.
21. Tu te fous de ce que pensent les autres.
22. T'aimes t'éclater avec tes copains.
23. Tu prends pas les autres pour des blaireaux.

a. You don't give a damn about what people think.
b. You are buried in work.
c. You don't take others for a ride.
d. You need to recharge batteries.
e. You really are an awesome guy.
f. You often put your foot in your mouth (it).
g. You have a very trendy style.
h. You are always dressed to kill.
i. You easily hit the roof.
j. You've had a haircut.
k. You look dead serious dressed up like that.
l. You love to have a laugh with your friends.
m. You cannot unwind after work.

C. Find the right word or expression from the list to end each sentence. (Only one correct answer for each sentence.)

une crise	**photo**	**dans le gaz**	**les dents**
au vinaigre	**long feu**	**un bide**	**ma claque**
forme	**saper**	**un coup de fil**	**tes batteries**
les dents	**mes gonds**	**dans les plumes**	

24. Ma bagnole tombe en panne tout le temps. Elle va pas tarder à me lâcher. Ça y a pas ______________.
25. T'as l'air crevé tu sais. Ça fait un an que tu bosses comme un forcené. Il serait temps que tu penses à recharger ________________.
26. Pour ton mariage, je vais me payer un nouveau costard. Ce jour-là, je vais vraiment bien me _______________.
27. Je rentre dans l'appart. Y avait un désordre pas croyable! Et Max qui fumait les pieds sur la table! Là, j'ai piqué ______________.
28. Ça faisait un moment qu'elle me prenait la tête. Mais quand elle m'a dit qu'elle invitait sa copine à s'installer chez nous, je suis sorti de ____________.

29. S'il continue à parler tout bas à Henri en me regardant dès que j'arrive au boulot, je sens que je vais lui voler ____________.
30. Au début, tout allait bien. On discutait des programmes de télé. Mais Marc s'est mis à parler politique et là très vite, entre lui et Cédric ça a tourné ___________.
31. Stéphanie a maigri, elle a une nouvelle coupe, elle fait du sport. Elle a vraiment l'air en pleine _________.
32. Paul fout rien de la journée. Quand je rentre c'est encore moi qui dois faire la bouffe. Je commence à en avoir _______.
33. On s'est défoncé pour monter cette pièce de théâtre. Mais la publicité était nulle, alors ça a été ___________.
34. Quelle soirée! Anne était crevée et Alain de mauvais poil. Pendant tout le dîner, il n'a pas desserré __________.
35. Ils ne se regardent pas, ils évitent de se parler. A mon avis c'est évident qu'entre eux, il y a de l'eau _____________.

D. The expressions underlined in the following sentences are slang and would only be used by close friends and in a very informal situation. Find from the list below the equivalent you could use safely in most situations, and rewrite the phrase, choosing the formal version from the list.

en colère	**te moquer de moi**	**s'en va**
porter sur les nerfs	**pleurer**	**des bêtises**
gâcher	**se disputer**	**se sâouler**

36. Je ne vais quand même pas foutre mes vacances en l'air à cause de ce repas de famille qui ne m'intéresse vraiment pas du tout!
37. Ça fait déjà la troisième fois cette semaine que tu me fais attendre pour rien. Est-ce que tu vas arrêter de te foutre de ma gueule?
38. Mon copain du Québec m'a dit hier qu'il était vraiment en sacrement après votre discussion hier soir à table.
39. Pour un soir de réveillon, bonjour l'ambiance! Stéphanie avait trop bu et elle a commencé à s'engueuler avec Julien.
40. Y a que des mecs bourrés dans cette boîte! Allez, on s'arrache!
41. Valérie venait de se faire plaquer par Simon. Elle a passé la soirée à chialer et à s'envoyer du whisky dans un coin.
42. La voir tchatcher tous les mecs qui passent, chaque fois qu'ils sortent, on sent bien que ça commence à le gonfler.

43. C'est pas possible. On dirait qu'il le fait exprès! Il conduit comme un dingue, se crashe avec sa voiture, il se bourre la gueule tous les soirs . . . il arrête pas de faire des conneries!

E. Choose the correct meaning for the following French words or expressions.

44. A friend from Quebec tells you that he is «brûlé». He means he is
    a. broke (skint).
    b. very tired.
    c. in trouble.

45. You are told that someone you know is «sur la paille». It means he
    a. has lost all his money.
    b. lives in the country.
    c. is in love.

46. You want to see a film. A friend tells you he's seen it and it is «un navet». It means:
    a. It's a great film.
    b. It's a funny film.
    c. It's a bad film.

47. If someone tells you «J'ai les crocs», it means that he is:
    a. angry.
    b. hungry.
    c. dizzy.

48. Friends raise their glasses and say to you «À la tienne». It means
    a. to your health.
    b. to your success.
    c. good luck.

49. If someone from Quebec says «J'en ai plein mon casque», he means
    a. I've had too much to drink.
    b. I've had as much as I can take.
    c. I have plenty of cash.

50. A friend tells you that Julien is «rétamé». He means
    a. he is really drunk.
    b. he is exhausted.
    c. he is bored.

Answers to Exercises

(À votre tour! and *Chapitres de révision)*

Chapitre 1

A. 1. g 2. f 3. e 4. a 5. h 6. c 7. d 8. b

B. 1. la gueule de bois 2. une piaule 3. la tronche 4. un rencard 5. pas de bol

C. 1. Bonjour 2. des tuyaux 3. Monsieur

Chapitre 2

A. 1. a 2. c 3. c 4. b

B. 1. Ils se sont faits rincer 2. je me casse 3. Il ne veut pas bouffer 4. On se les gèle 5. faut pas pousser 6. Il en a rien à foutre 7. c'est le comble

C. 1. Ça fait vingt minutes qu'on poireaute. 2. Je vous avais dit qu'on était à la bourre. 3. Y a de l'abus. 4. C'est quoi ça? 5. C'est complètement cramé. 6. Faut pas pousser quand même. 7. Vous savez qu'il y a des gens qui poireautent?

D. 1. Je poireaute (g) 2. C'est une blague (f) 3. ça marche? (e) 4. Y a pas l'feu (b) 5. papoter (h) 6. rien à foutre (d) 7. péter un plomb (c) 8. dingue (a)

Chapitre 3

A. 1. a 2. a 3. b 4. b 5. a

B. 1. c 2. e 3. g 4. f 5. i 6. h 7. a 8. b 9. d

C.
M: perdu
MME: Ne te fais pas de souci / monsieur / aimable
M: Est-ce que vous pourriez nous dire où se trouve la gare, s'il vous plaît?
PASSANT: Malheureusement, je ne suis pas d'ici.
M: Très bien! / difficile
MME: Au revoir, et merci, monsieur.

D. 1. Excusez-moi, Monsieur, vous sauriez où est l'Office de Tourisme? 2. Désolé, je ne peux pas vous renseigner. 3. Je suis juste de passage ici. 4. Ça ne me revient pas. 5. C'est pas la porte à côté! 6. Le café vient juste de fermer. 7. Tournez à gauche, prenez le bus H et descendez au CHU. 8. Ça n'a pas l'air d'être trop balèze à trouver.

Chapitre 4

A. 1. f 2. g 3. e 4. c 5. b 6. d 7. a

B. 1. e 2. h 3. g 4. a 5. b 6. c 7. f 8. d

C. 1. un rond 2. plein aux as 3. tombe à pic 4. c'est vraiment un pote 5. de la gratte 6. me faire suer 7. chouette 8. frangin 9. mon blé

D. 1. Il ne faut pas 2. Tu n'as pas 3. Je n'ai pas 4. Je ne te l'ai pas 5. Tu n'as qu'à 6. Tu n'es pas 7. Il y a 8. Tu ne crois pas?

E. 1. T'as qu'à / ta gratte / faire la manche 2. vois venir / tes gros sabots 3. T'es bouché? 4. me faire suer 5. frangin / plein aux as

Chapitres de révision 1–4

A.

							[1]S				
			[2]T			[3]C	A	S	S	É	E
		[4]B	O	[5]F			L				
	[6]P	O	I	R	E	[7]A	U	T	E	R	
		N		A		S	T				
		J		N		S					[8]P
[9]B		O		G		U					I
O		U		I		R					A
U		R		N		E			[10]C	R	U
L						R			U		L
E									I		E
[11]S	Y	M	P	A					[12]T	E	S

B. 15. i 16. d 17. j 18. f 19. g 20. h 21. e 22. c 23. b 24. a

C. 25. péter un plomb 26. râler 27. se les gèle 28. la gueule de bois 29. crâmé 30. bouffe 31. cuites 32. me casse 33. du bol 34. s'éclater

D. 35. e 36. c 37. a 38. i 39. b 40. d 41. f 42. g

E. 43. a 44. b 45. c 46. a 47. c 48. c 49. a 50. b

Chapitre 5

A. 1. d 2. e 3. f 4. a 5. h 6. i 7. c 8. b 9. g

B. 1. d 2. c 3. f 4. g 5. h 6. b 7. i 8. e 9. a

C. 1. J'ai le moral à zéro 2. me lâcher 3. A la teuf 4. Il m'a posé un lapin 5. chopé la crève 6. passait en coup de vent 7. des bobards 8. Il s'est bien payé ma tronche 9. Marc était cassé 10. comater 11. mener en bateau

D. 1. mon assiette / la crève 2. une teuf / une combine / des bobards 3. moral à zéro / ils y vont un peu fort 4. payé ma tronche 5. sourdingue / payer un râteau 6. broyer du noir / tout un plat / déprime

Chapitre 6

A. 1. à l'ouest (f) 2. débouler (g) 3. faucher (a) 4. chômé (b) 5. dépouiller (h) 6. que dalle (d) 7. bourré (e) 8. flipper à mort (c)

B. 1. c 2. d 3. g 4. b 5. a 6. f 7. c 8. h 9. e

C. a. 1. Je suis tombé dans la rue. 2. Les passants riaient. 3. On m'a volé mon porte-feuille. 4. J'ai vraiment pas eu de chance. b. 1. Je me suis cassé la gueule dans la rue. 2. Les passants se fendaient la gueule. 3. On m'a fauché mon porte-feuille. 4. J'ai vraiment pas eu de bol.

D. 1. piquer 2. flipper à mort 3. racailles 4. dépouillé 5. baraqués 6. que dalle 7. caisse 8. défoncer 9. pas large 10. files 11. buter

Chapitre 7

A. 1. marre 2. faible 3. bail 4. craquant 5. baratiner 6. films 7. solide 8. lâche

B. 1. b 2. b 3. a 4. a 5. a 6. a 7. a 8. b

C. 1. tirer la gueule (h) 2. à côté de la plaque (g) 3. pousse un peu (e) 4. me faire une scène (f) 5. un bail (c) 6. sacré culot (b) 7. plié de rire (a) 8. on s'éclate (d)

D. 1. Arrête de mater la nana là-bas! 2. Te monte pas la tête! 3. Si on sortait en boîte tous les deux? 4. J'ai vraiment un gros faible pour toi. 5. J'ai flashé sur lui dès que je l'ai vu. 6. Je suis vraiment accro. 7. Entre nous deux, c'est du solide.

Chapitre 8

A. 1. guindé 2. dégueu 3. mouchoir de poche 4. glauque 5. crade 6. tape-à-l'oeil 7. boucan 8. hyper-bondé

B. 1. largué 2. je-m'en-foutiste 3. foutue 4. bourré 5. aguichante 6. marrant 7. rigolard 8. bourge

C. 1. dégoté (b) 2. s'empiffrent (a) 3. foutait (h) 4. partante (g) 5. se ramène (f) 6. du gâteau (c) 7. se concocter (d) 8. bourge (e)

D. 1. décontract 2. calme 3. grand comme un mouchoir de poche 4. crade 5. glauque 6. aguichante 7. je-m'en-foutiste 8. bourge

Chapitre 9

A. 1. f 2. e 3. d 4. c 5. g 6. a 7. b

B. 1. Non! C'était galère! 2. Moi? Je suis une bille en anglais. 3. Avec une vraie bombe suédoise. 4. J'étais sur le cul. 5. de la muscu trois fois par semaine. 6. Tu te casses. 7. Oui, ça fait un bail.

C. 1. marre 2. en quatre 3. pomper 4. des vannes 5. aux baskets 6. croix dessus 7. prends/tête

D. 1. J'ai le blues. 2. Je suis sorti avec une fille carrément canon. 3. Je l'ai draguée dans une boîte. 4. Il/Elle rapplique tout le temps. 5. Il/Elle me pompe l'air! 6. Arrête de m'envoyer des vannes. 7. Je vais devoir faire une croix dessus.

Chapitres de révision 5–9

A.

1 C		2 G				3 V			4 B
5 A	G	U	I	6 C	H	A	N	T	E
I		I		O					C
S		N		N			7 F		A
S		D			8 C	U	L		N
E		E			H		I		E
					O		P		
9 M	A	X			M		P		
E					E		E		
10 C	O	L	L	E	R		R		

B. 13. e 14. n 15. f 16. h 17. d 18. g 19. a 20. i 21. b 22. k 23. m 24. c 25. l 26. j

C. 27. accro 28. bourré 29. pompes 30. la crève 31. leurrer 32. flipper 33. une croix 34. piquer 35. lâcher 36. fringues

D. 37. Il était complètement à l'ouest 38. à broyer du noir 39. se fait dépouiller 40. Il est passé en coup de vent 41. J'en menais pas large 42. les bras m'en sont tombés 43. Je ne me fais pas de films

E. 44. a 45. b 46. c 47. a 48. b 49. b 50. b

Chapitre 10

A. 1. fourgué 2. se trimbaler 3. tiendra le coup 4. une virée 5. galère 6. occulté 7. blaireau 8. y a pas photo

B. 1. b 2. b 3. b 4. a 5. a 6. b 7. a 8. b

C. 1. i 2. h 3. e 4. g 5. d 6. b 7. f 8. a 9. c

D. 1. J'irai bien faire une petite virée en Belgique. 2. J'ai un boulot d'enfer actuellement. 3. Je me suis complètement investi dans mon travail. 4. On fourgue les planches dans la voiture de Guillaume. 5. On pourrait y aller à bécane.

Chapitre 11

A. 1. b 2. a 3. a 4. a 5. b 6. a 7. a

B. 1. les tifs (f) 2. les boules (g) 3. chouette (e) 4. m'aurais vu (h) 5. s'éclate (b) 6. décrocher (d) 7. sa claque (a) 8. tourné au vinaigre (c)

C. 1. e 2. g 3. a 4. f 5. c 6. b 7. h 8. d

D. 1. C'est vraiment super cette nouvelle coiffure. 2. T'as l'air en pleine forme! 3. Tu es drôlement bien sapé ce matin. 4. C'est sympa de me dire ça. 5. Tu fais carrément sérieux comme ça. 6. Félicitations! 7. Ça te donne un look beaucoup plus cool. 8. C'est chouette de te revoir.

Chapitre 12

A. 1. râpé (c) 2. faux-derche (d) 3. sape le moral (e) 4. péter les plombs. (a) 5. foutu nos vacances en l'air (b)

B. 1. Q 2. Q 3. F 4. Q 5. Q 6. F 7. Q 8. Q 9. Q

C. 1. a 2. b 3. a 4. a 5. a 6. b 7. a

D. 1. J'y crois! C'est vraiment trop nul! Tu plaisantes? 2. Écoute, j'ai une grosse galère. 3. Non, laisse tomber. 4. Moi, si ça m'était arrivé, j'aurais pété des plombs. 5. Tu sais, moi, je suis sûr que c'est un faux-derche, ce mec. 6. Cette date de mariage, ça va me foutre mes vacances en l'air! 7. Je sais que j'aurai du fun si je venais, mais je suis vraiment trop brûlé ce soir.

Chapitre 13

A. 1. d 2. f 3. g 4. a 5. h 6. e 7. c 8. b

B. 1. nul / mauvais / de la daube 2. un bide complet / un échec 3. minables / mauvais / nuls 4. j'en avais ma claque / j'en avais marre / je me suis ennuyé 5. nul / inintéressant / ennuyeux 6. avait pas l'air dans son assiette / avait pas l'air bien 7. ne va pas faire long feu / ne va pas durer longtemps 8. n'a pas desserré les dents / dit un mot

C. 1. c'est nul 2. j'en ai assez 3. c'est fichu 4. on s'est disputés 5. faire la tête 6. gâché mon argent 7. c'est dur 8. c'est excitant 9. je rêve 10. des bêtises

D. 1. Avec Anne, on a passé la journée à s'engueuler. 2. C'est vraiment foutre son fric par la fenêtre d'acheter ce CD. 3. T'as pas trouvé que la teuf hier c'était nul? 4. Écoute, c'est franchement délire le film que je viens de voir! 5. T'as pas desserré les dents pendant la teuf. Qu'est-ce qui tournait pas rond? 6. Ce roman est un navet et j'ai rien capté de l'histoire. 7. Arrête de dire des conneries. 8. Tu veux rigoler là quand tu dis que cette pièce, c'est de la daube?

Chapitre 14

A. 1. h 2. e 3. f 4. g 5. c 6. b 7. a 8. d

B. 1. magne-toi 2. j'ai vraiment la dalle 3. j'ai une ardoise 4. becter 5. mousse 6. un vrai pochtron 7. j'étais complètement rétamé 8. elle crache pas sur l'apéro

C. 1. Ça s'arrose! 2. On se prend un p'tit apéro? 3. Allez, on trinque tous à Julien. 4. A la tienne 5. Félicitations! 6. A ton nouveau boulot!

D. 1. (I) Je n'aime pas l'eau. Je ne bois que du vin. 2. (F) Il a l'air complètement rétamé. 3. (F) Ça va nous coûter la peau des fesses. 4. (I) On va s'offrir un bon repas. 5. (I) Allez, on reprend un autre verre. 6. (I) J'ai terriblement faim. 7. (I) Il boit et après, il est de mauvaise humeur. 8. (F) Lui, on voit qu'il a une sacrée descente.

Chapitres de révision 10–14

A.

	[1]H	A	L	L	U	[2]C	I	N	E	R	
						O					[3]G
			[4]T	H	U	N	E	S			A
			E			N					L
	[5]A		U		[6]M	E	U	L	E		E
	R		F			R					R
	R					I			[7]T		E
[8]F	O	U	R	[9]G	U	E	R		I		
	S			O		S			F		[10]C
	E			N					S		L
	R			D							O
			[11]A	S	S	U	R	E	R		U

B. 13. e 14. g 15. h 16. j 17. b 18. d 19. m 20. i 21. a 22. l 23. c

C. 24. photo 25. tes batteries 26. saper 27. une crise 28. mes gonds 29. dans les plumes 30. au vinaigre 31. forme 32. ma claque 33. un bide 34. les dents 35. dans le gaz

D. 36. gâcher mes vacances. 37. arrêter de te moquer de moi? 38. Il était vraiment en colère. 39. à se disputer. 40. on s'en va. 41. à pleurer. 42. à lui porter sur les nerfs. 43. il se saoûle/de faire des bêtises.

E. 44. b 45. a 46. c 47. b 48. a 49. b 50. a

French-English Glossary

The numbers in brackets refer to the chapter(s) in which the word or expression appears in the **Conversations, Attention au langage familier!** sections, or **Histoires drôles.** Terms that are explained in more detail in **Language and Culture** sections are marked [L&C]. An asterisk indicates vulgarity (see Introduction, page viii).

à côté de la plaque way off the mark [7]
à l'ouest completely lost [6]
à la bourre running late [2]
à la tienne/à la vôtre Cheers! [14]
à sec cleaned out (without a bean) [4]
abus: Y a de l'abus. That's going too far! [2]
Abuse pas! Don't push your luck! [1, 4]
abuser to exaggerate [13]
accro hooked, attached to [L&C 7]
un accro du web fan of the Web [L&C 9]
accrocher to get hooked on something [11]
une adresse électronique E-mail address [L&C 9]
une adresse E-mail E-mail address [L&C 9]
aguichante enticing, attractive [8]
aller: y aller fort to go over the top [5]
aller en boîte to go clubbing [9]
une ambiance atmosphere [8]
Amène-toi! Come here! [3]
une andouille fool (sort of sausage) [14]
annoncer la couleur to come clean, to put one's cards on the table [4]
un apéro (= apéritif) drink, aperitif [14, L&C 14]
un appart(ement) apartment (flat) [8]
une ardoise: avoir une ardoise to have a tab (slate) [14, L&C 14]
arobase @ [L&C 9]
arroser to celebrate with a drink [14]
assiette: dans son assiette feeling good [5]
assurer to know exactly what has to be done [3, 10]
au fin fond in the depths of [11]

un auteur author [8]
une aventure adventure, affair [L&C 7]
aveugle blind [6]
avoir du bol to be lucky (in luck) [6]
avoir les moyens de payer to be able to afford it [4]

la bagnole car, automobile [10]
le bail long time, age(s) (yonks) [7, 9]
le baiser kiss [7, L&C 7]
baiser* to fuck [7, L&C 7]
baladeuses: (des mains) baladeuses wandering (hands) [13]
balèse: être balèse (to be) difficult (also spelled **balèze**) [3]
la balle franc [4, 12]
la banlieue suburb [5, L&C 5]
baraqué heavily built, muscular, hefty, well-built (hunky) [6, 9]
le baratin chat [11]
baratiner to hit on (to chat up) [7]
les baskets gym shoes (trainers), basketball shoes [9, L&C 9]
le bâton stick, 10,000 francs [4]
BCBG (= bon chic bon genre) middle-class, bourgeois [L&C 9]
la bécane computer, motorbike [9, L&C 9, 10]
becter to eat, to chow (to nosh) [13, 14, L&C 14]
ben (= bien) well [1]
béton fixed, solid, firm [10, 12]
béton (= tomber) to fall (**verlan**) [L&C 5]
le/la beur (= arabe) young Arab (**verlan**) [5, L&C 5]
le bide failure [13]
bien fait decent food [L&C 14]
bien foutue with a lovely body [8]
bien sapé very sharp [11]
bien tassé: (un whisky bien tassé) a good measure (of whisky) [6]
la bille block [9]
les binocles glasses, spectacles [8]
la bise kiss [11]
la bise: faire la bise to kiss (on both cheeks) [1]
le bistro bistro [L&C 14]
la blague joke [2]
un blaireau poor sap [10]
la blanquette (de veau) blanquette of veal [L&C 14]
blaster to blast [L&C 5]

le blé money, cash, wealth [4]
la blonde pale ale [L&C 14]
le blues depression, blues [9]
le bobard lie, fib [5]
le bock glass of beer, drink, brew (bevy) [6]
bof expression meaning "not too well," "so-so" [1]
boire un canon to have a glass of wine [L&C 14]
boire un coup to have a drink [L&C 14]
boire un demi to have a half a beer [L&C 14]
la boîte nightclub [7, 9]
la boîte d'allumettes box of matches [9]
la boîte de nuit nightclub [9]
bol: (pas de) bol (no) luck [3, 12]
bol: avoir du bol to be in luck [1]
la bombe bombshell [9]
Bonjour! Hello! (*see page 98*) [8]
la bonne bouffe good food [L&C 14]
Bonsoir messieurs-dames. Evening, everybody. [3]
booster to give support, to make someone feel better [5, L&C 5]
bosser to work (hard) [4, 13]
le boucan racket, row [8]
bouché stupid [4]
boucler to finish (a job) [10]
la bouffe food, meal, something to eat, grub (nosh) (fodder) [1, 8, 14]
bouffer to eat, to have a meal, to chow (to nosh) [2, 14, L&C 14]
la bouillebaisse bouillebaisse (fish stew) [L&C 14]
les boules francs [4], bad luck [12]
les boules: avoir les boules to be scared [11]
le boulot work, job [10]
le bouquet bunch of flowers, high point [13]
le bouquin book [8]
bourge(ois) middle class [8]
le bourge yuppie [12]
bourre: être à la bourre to be (running) late [1, 2]
bourré drunk [6, 8]
un bout de temps quite a while [1]
brancher to appeal, to turn on [10]
Les bras m'en sont tombés. I was absolutely amazed. [6]
le brique brick, 10,000 francs [4, 10]
broncher to move a muscle [13]

broyer du noir to be down in the dumps, to be depressed [5]
brûlé tired (**québécois**) [12]
la brune brown ale [L&C 14]
buter to kill [6]

C'est à l'eau. It's ruined. It's all off. [12]
C'est balèze! It's great! It's a real problem! [9]
C'est cadeau. It's a treat. [14]
C'est clair. That's for sure. [6]
C'est du sérieux. It's really serious. [7, L&C 7]
C'est du solide. It's serious. It's the real thing. [L&C 7]
C'est fichu. It's ruined. It's all off. [12]
C'est foutu. It's ruined. It's all off. [12]
C'est kif kif. It's all the same. [L&C 5]
C'est le pied! It's absolutely the best! [L&C 7]
C'est pas de mon âge. I'm too old for that. [3]
C'est pas la porte à côté. It's not next door. [3]
C'est quoi ça? What's this? [2]
C'est vache! That's terrible! That sucks! (That's a real pig!) [5]
Ça craint un max. That really sucks. It's the pits. [12]
Ça fait un bail. It's been ages. [11]
Ça marche? Is that all right? Is that acceptable? [2]
Ça me les gonfle.* It pisses me off. [11]
Ça me sape le moral. That really gets me down. [12]
Ça me scie. I'm really shocked (literally: "That saws me in half.") [6]
Ça ne me revient pas. I can't remember. [3]
Ça s'arrose! That deserves a drink! [11, 14, L&C 14]
Ça va craindre. It'll be difficult. [10]
Ça va? How are things? How are you doing? [1]
le cadre executive [10]
cafouiller to mess things up (to make a balls of something) [2]
la caisse car, automobile [10]
le câlin cuddle, caress [7, L&C 7]
camé high (on drugs) [10]
canon marvelous, terrific, the tops [9]
le canon drink [14]
le caoutchouc rubber (for instance, a contraceptive) [4]
capter to understand, to grasp the meaning [13]
carrément absolutely, totally, really, very [9, 11]
la casquette cap [9, L&C 9]

cassé ill, unwell, totally exhausted [5]
casser to break up [11]
casser la croûte to have a meal [L&C 14]
casser la dalle to have a meal [L&C 14]
casser la graine to have a meal [L&C 14]
casser les pieds (à quelqu'un) to bore somebody to death [L&C 7]
la casse-tête difficult problem [8]
Cassos. Let's go. [8]
le cassoulet cassoulet [L&C 14]
castrer to castrate [8]
le CD-ROM (cédérom) CD-ROM [L&C 9]
CDI contract with no fixed term [11]
le cédérom (CD-ROM) CD-ROM [9]
le céfran (= français) (**verlan**) [5, L&C 5]
CGT (= Conféderation générale du travail) Association of French Trade Unions [L&C 9]
le/la CGTiste member of the CGT [L&C 9]
le char car, automobile (**québécois**) [10]
charrier to push things too far, to exaggerate [5]
chébran (= branché) (**verlan**) [5, L&C 5]
chialer to shout, to scream, to weep [7, L&C 7, 11]
chiant* boring [8]
chier* to shit [8]
la chierie* something really tedious [8]
la chignole car, automobile [10]
la chiotte motorbike (mobylette) [10]
chômer to be out of work, to hang around (about) [6]
le chômeur someone unemployed [L&C 9]
choper la crève to catch a chill [5]
choper to catch [2]
la choucroute choucroute, sauerkraut [L&C 14]
chouette super, great, marvelous [4]
chouffer to look [L&C 5]
chouraver to steal [5, L&C 5]
le CHU (= Centre Hospitalier Urbain) a hospital [3]
le ciné cinema, pictures, movies [4]
le cinoche cinema, movies [4]
claqué exhausted [12]
claque: en avoir sa claque to have as much as you can take [13]
le clochard tramp [L&C 9]

la cloche: se taper la cloche to have a good meal [14]
le clou nail, old junker (banger) [10]
la cohabitation living together [7, L&C 7]
coin: être du coin to come from, to live in the area/district [3]
coller to stick, to last [6, 9]
coller à to stick to [12]
comater to be passed out, to be fast asleep [5]
le comble the absolute limit [2]
le commerçant businessman [4]
la compagne female partner [7, L&C 7]
le compagnon male partner [7, L&C 7]
le compte bank account [10]
con* stupid [10, 12]
connaître: On se connaît? Have we met? [14]
le connard* jerk, fool, idiot (twat, berk) [11, 12]
les conneries* stupid action, stupid statement; trash (rubbish, balls) [12, 13]
la convivialité social interaction, conviviality [L&C 14]
cool cool, awesome [7, 11]
les cordes: gratter les cordes to play the guitar [4]
le costard suit [11]
costard-cravate dressed formally [11]
costume-cravate dressed formally [11]
côté: à côté de la plaque way off the mark [7]
coucher avec to bed, to sleep with [L&C 7]
le coup de blanc white wine [L&C 14]
le coup de rouge red wine [L&C 14]
le coup de vache dirty trick [8]
couper: ne pas y couper to not miss [14]
le couple cohabitant couple living together [L&C 7, L&C 9]
le courrier él E-mail address [L&C 9]
le couscous couscous [L&C 14]
coûter (la peau des fesses*) to cost (an arm and a leg) [14]
cracher (sur quelque chose) to say no to, to spit on [14]
crade filthy [8]
cradingue filthy [8]
crado filthy [8]
cramer to go up in smoke, to burn [2]
craquant gorgeous, hot [7]
craquer to give way, to weaken [9]
crasseux filthy [8]

la crêpe crêpe, pancake [L&C 14]
crevé exhausted [12]
crever (de faim) to die (of hunger) [5, 14]
crocs: avoir les crocs to be famished [14]
croire dur comme fer to be absolutely convinced [6]
la croix cross [9]
la croûte: casser la croûte to have a meal, snack [14]
cru raw, uncooked [11]
la cuisine cooking [14]
la cuisine du terroir regional dishes [14, L&C 14]
la cuisine régionale regional dishes [L&C 14]
le cuistot chef [14]
cuit cooked [11]
la cuite (prendre une cuite) (to get) drunk [1]
le cul* ass (arse) [9]
le cul*: être comme cul et chemise to be thick with someone (to be as thick as thieves) [9]
le culot nerve (cheek) [7]
culotté: être culotté to have a lot of nerve (cheek) [7]
la culture culture [L&C 5]
le cybercafé cybercafé [L&C 9]

dalle: avoir la dalle to be hungry [14]
la daube trash (rubbish) [13]
dealer to deal (drugs) [L&C 5]
débordé: être débordé to be overwhelmed (usually by work) [2]
débouler to turn up quite unexpectedly [6]
déconner* to talk absolute trash (rubbish) [12]
décontract(é) relaxed, chilled-out, mellow [8]
décrocher to unwind, to relax, to take the phone off the hook [11]
défoncer to smash in [6]
dégoter to find [8]
dégueu(lasse)* disgusting [8]
déjeuner to have lunch (*also* to have breakfast) [L&C 14]
délire dreamy, great, marvelous [9, 13]
délirer to be crazy [12]
délirer: Tu délires! You've got to be joking! You can't be serious! [6]
démarrer to start work, to get going (starting a car) [2]
déphasé out of synch, out of touch [11]
dépouiller to strip off, to rob [6]

des tomates en boîte canned (tinned) tomatoes [9]
une descente: avoir une descente to knock it back [14]
desserrer les dents to unclench one's teeth [13]
dingue crazy, mad [2, 5, 7]
dire des nouvelles *see notes on page 18* [2]
dis donc tell me, say [1]
la disquette floppy disk [9, L&C 9]
le dossier file [L&C 9]
la drague hitting on (chatting up), pick-up, cruising [7, L&C 7]
draguer to hit on (to chat up), to pick up [7, L&C 7]
le dragueur woman-chaser [L&C 7]
dur difficult [9]

eau: Il y a de l'eau dans le gaz. Things are not running smoothly. [13]
écluser to throw back (to sink) one's drink [14]
une école hôtellière catering school [L&C 14]
Elle est très cul.* She's really keen on it. [9]
Elle me mène en bateau. She's taking me for a ride. [5]
Elle se paye ma tronche. She's making fun of me. She's jerking me around. (She's taking the piss.) [5]
emballer to pick up [7, L&C 7]
embaucher to hire, to take a job [8]
embêter: T'embête pas. Don't get worked up about it. [3]
un embout de caoutchouc a rubber tip (on the end of a walking stick) [4]
embrasser to kiss [L&C 7]
émerger to emerge, to get to the end of a job [10]
en avoir marre to have as much as you can take [12]
en avoir plein son casque to have as much as you can take (**québécois**) [12]
en avoir sa claque to have as much as you can take [11]
en chier* to bust a gut [8]
en coup de vent in a hurry [5]
en faire tout un plat to make a big deal about something (to make a meal of something) [5]
en ligne on-line [9, L&C 9]
en masse plenty, masses (**québécois**) [12]
en pleine forme in (on) top form [11]
engueuler to yell at somebody [L&C 7]
envoyer des vannes to make spiteful remarks [9]
estomac: avoir l'estomac dans les talons to be very hungry [14]

être comme cul et chemise to be thick with someone (to be as thick as thieves) [9]

être en calvaire to be angry (**québécois**) [12]

être en hostie to be angry (**québécois**) [12]

être en maudit to be angry (**québécois**) [12]

être en sacrement to be furious (**québécois**) [12]

être furax to be really mad [12]

un/une ex ex-partner, old flame [11]

le faible (avoir un faible pour) weak spot (to have a soft spot for) [7, L&C 7]

faire chier to be totally boring [L&C 7]

faire chier quelqu'un to annoy, to make trouble (to give grief) [4]

faire des films to invent a drama [7]

faire du pied to play footsie [13]

faire la bombe to have fun, to have a ball [12]

faire de gaffe to put one's foot in one's mouth [2]

faire la manche to beg, to ask for money (to busk) [4, L&C 9]

faire long feu to hang fire, to last [13]

faire sortir de ses gonds to make somebody mad [11]

faire suer to annoy, to bore, to bug, to make trouble (to give grief) [4]

faire: T'en fais pas. Don't worry about it. Don't let it bother you. (Don't go on about it.) [5]

faire une croix dessus to bring to an end [9]

faire une scène to create a scene [7]

la famille nombreuse large family [4]

le fast food fast food [L&C 14]

fauché cleaned out (skint) [4]

faucher to steal, to rip off (to nick) [6]

Faut pas pousser. Don't push your luck. [13]

le faux-derche hypocrite [12]

fermer la gueule (à quelqu'un) to shut somebody's mouth [12]

le festivalier festival-goer [L&C 9]

la fête festival, celebration [L&C 14]

feu: Y pas l' feu! No rush! Calm down! [2]

filer to give [4, 6], to slip (money) [13]

filer (un rencard) to make a date [1]

flasher to spark, to fall head over heels [7]

le flic cop, police [5]

flippé high (on drugs) [10]

flipper (à mort) to get (totally) stressed out [6]
le flyer publicity flyer [L&C 9]
la forme: tenir la forme to be in good shape [13]
fourguer to sell, to hand over (to flog) [10]
fourré hanging out (holed up) [8]
Fous-moi la paix! Leave me alone! Give me a break! [4]
foutre en l'air to ruin completely [12]
foutre le camp* to leave, to beat it (to sod off) [4, 10]
foutre par la fenêtre* to throw out of the window, to throw down the drain [13]
foutre* (Qu'est-ce qu'il fout*? en avoir rien à foutre*) to do [2]
frais: aux frais de . . . at the expense of . . . ; . . . is paying [2]
la francophonie parts of the world where French is spoken [12]
le frangin brother [4]
le fric cash, loot, dough [4, 5, 6]
les fringues clothes [6]
friqué loaded, wealthy [4]
les fruits de mer seafood [14, L&C 14]
le fun: avoir du fun to have fun (**québécois**) [12]
le fun: C'est pour le fun. It's for fun, pleasure. [12]
furax really mad [2]
la fute trousers, slacks, pants (strides) [6, 8]

le gaffeur someone who keeps putting his foot in his mouth [11]
la galère difficulty [12]
galère difficult (hard going) [10]
la gang group of friends (**québécois**) [12]
le gars guy (bloke, lad) [4]
gâteau: C'est du gâteau. It's a piece of cake. [8]
gaulois bawdy [7, L&C 7]
génial terrific, marvelous, brilliant, **chouette** [4, 8]
le gigot leg of lamb [14, L&C 14]
glauque sad place [8]
gober to swallow whole [7]
les godasses shoes, footwear [6]
gonflé: être gonflé to have a lot of nerve (cheek) [7]
gonfler to bore [L&C 7], to exasperate, to annoy [11]
la gratte guitar [4]
gratteux mean, miserly (**québécois**) [12]
grave really (when used as an adverb) [2]; serious(ly) [14]

grignoter to nibble [L&C 14]
grillé ruined [13]
la gueule features, face [8]
la gueule de bois hangover [1]
guindé stiff, starchy, uptight [8]

halluciner to fantasize [13]
le hamburger hamburger [L&C 14]
la hauteur height [8]
l'hosto (= hôpital) hospital [10]
hyper bien couldn't be better [7]
hyper-bondé packed full [8]

un impair blunder, gaffe [11]
un imper(méable) raincoat [2]
improviser to make something up [10]
intello (= intellectuel) intellectual [9]
un/une internaute web surfer [L&C 9]
l'internet Internet [9, L&C 9]

J'te dis pas! You just can't imagine! [10]
jasant chatty (**québécois**) [12]
jaune: un p'tit jaune pastis [14]
je-m'en-foutiste someone who doesn't give a damn about anything [8]
Je me demande si vous pourriez . . . I wonder if you could possibly . . . [3]
Je me la fais. I get her into bed. [9]
Je me taperai bien . . . I would really like to eat . . . [L&C 14]
Je n'en menais pas large. My stomach was all in knots. (My heart was in my boots.) [6]
Je te vois venir . . . avec tes gros sabots. I can see through you. [4]
jeter: s'en jeter un* to down a drink [14]
la job work (**québécois**), temporary work [12]
le joint joint [L&C 5]
le joual slang term for **québécois** [12]
jouir to come, to hit the heights (sexually) [7]
le jules guy (bloke), man, lover, partner, husband [6, L&C 7]

le keuf (= flic) police (**verlan**) [5, L&C 5]
le keus (= sac) bag (**verlan**) [L&C 5]
kiffant great, terrific [L&C 5, 10]

lâcher to leave [5], to dump (drop) someone [7, L&C 7]; to release [12]
lâcher son fou to have a great time (**québécois**) [12]
la langue language, tongue [L&C 5]
la langue des banlieues language of the suburbs [L&C 5]
largué spaced out, not with it (all at sea) [8]
leurrer to deceive [5]
la lèvre lip [L&C 9]
la librairie bookshop [8]
limoger to fire (give the sack) [8]
linker to seduce [L&C 5]
le logiciel software [L&C 9]
le look look, style, appearance [L&C 9]
lourder to kick out [8]
lourder: se faire lourder to be fired (to get the sack) [8]
les lumières ideas (**On a besoin de tes lumières,** "We need to pick your brain.") [3]

magner/se magner to get a move on [14]
mailer to E-mail, to send an E-mail [9, L&C 9]
manchot one-armed (or, sometimes, without arms) [6]
marche: Ça marche. It's OK. It's fine. [1]
marché: par dessus l'marché to top it all (to crown it all) [2]
marrant(e) good fun, a bit of a laugh [8]
marre: en avoir marre to be sick of something, to have as much as you can take, to be fed up with [2, 7]
mater to eye up [7, L&C 7]
le max(imum) the most, absolutely, maximum [3, 9]
le mec guy (bloke) [6, L&C 7, 8]
le mel E-mail [L&C 9]
Merde alors! Shit! Damn! (Bugger!) [3]
messieurs: Bonsoir messieurs-dames. Evening, everybody. [3]
mettre dans le coup to convince, to win over [8]
la meuf (= femme) woman (**verlan**) [L&C 5]
la meule motorbike [10]
mignon sweet, cute [5]
minable pathetic [13]
minauder to mince, to simper [11]
monter la tête to get angry, mad [7]
le moral morale [5]
mortel marvelous! [11]

le mouchoir (de poche) (pocket) handkerchief [8]
la mousse beer [14, L&C 14]
la muscu(lation) bodybuilding [9]

la nana girl, woman, chick (bird) [5, L&C 5, L&C 7]
la narine nostril [L&C 9]
le narzo (= zonard) dropout, seasonal traveler (**verlan**) [L&C 9]
nase exhausted [12], feeble [13]
le navet turnip, turkey (failed play/film) [13]
le net Internet [L&C 9]
Ni vu ni connu! You wouldn't even know anything had happened! [6]
nouvelles news (*see notes on page 18*) [2]
nouvelles: Il aura de mes nouvelles. I'll give him a piece of my mind. [2]
nul zero, worthless [9]

une occase (= occasion) occasion [14]
occulter to shut out completely [10]
On s'est fait chier.* We were bored out of our minds. [8]
un ordinateur computer [L&C 9]
une oreille ear [L&C 9]
ouest: à l'ouest completely lost [6]
outré outraged [13]

un p'tit jaune pastis [L&C 14]
PACS (= Pacte civile de solidarité) PACS law (law giving equal rights to all couples) [L&C 7, L&C 9]
pacser to form a couple according to the PACS law [L&C 7, L&C 9]
la page web webpage [L&C 9]
la paille straw, **sur la paille** = penniless [10]
papoter to chatter [2]
parler: Tu parles! So what! [4]
partant ready and willing, up for it, keen [8, 10]
pas dans son assiette not feeling quite oneself, a bit off color [4]
pas de bol out of luck [1, 13]
passage: être de passage to be passing through [3]
passer bien to be well suited [8]
passer un coup de fil to call, to phone [10]
un pastis pastis [L&C 14]
paumer quelque chose to lose something [3]
pauvre gars poor fool (sod) [6]

peloter to caress, to fondle, to feel (touch) up [7, L&C 7, 13]
le pépin glitch (hitch), snag [6]
un pernod pastis [L&C 14]
péter des plombs to blow your top [12]
péter un plomb to blow a fuse (to bust a gut) [2]
péter to blow up, to fart, to break down [2]
photo: Y a pas photo. It's obvious. You're absolutely right. [10]
la piaule room, pad (digs) [1]
la picole boozing [14]
picoler to tipple [L&C 14]
pied: C'est le pied! It's absolutely the best! [7]
le piercing body-piercing [L&C 9]
piger to understand [1]
le pinard cheap wine (plonk) [14, L&C 14]
piquer une crise to throw a fit [11]
piquer to steal, to rip off (to nick) [6]
la pizzeria pizzeria [L&C 14]
placoter to chatter (**québécois**) [12]
le plaisir pleasure [L&C 14]
le plan plan [10]
plan: un bon plan a good idea [10]
plaquer to dump (to drop) a partner [L&C 7, 9, 11]
plate: C'était plate. It was a pity. (**québécois**) [12]
plein aux as well off, loaded [4]
pleuvoir (des cordes) to pour with rain [2]
plier de rire to wet oneself (crease oneself) laughing [7]
le pochtron drunkard, heavy drinker (piss artist) [14, L&C 14]
le pognon cash, loot, dough [4]
un poil a tiny bit (literally "a hair") [2]
poil: être de bon/mauvais poil to be in a good/bad mood [14]
poil: n'avancer pas d'un poil to advance hardly at all [14]
poil: reprendre du poil de la bête to recover (from a hangover) [14]
poireau: faire le poireau to hang around (about) [2]
poireauter to be kept waiting, to hang around [2]
le poivrot heavy drinker, drunkard [14, L&C 14]
pomper (l'air) to pump (air), to bug someone [9]
les pompes shoes, sports shoes [6 ,11]
porter à l'envers to wear back to front [L&C 9]
poser un lapin to stand up, to leave in the lurch [5]
le pot-au-feu hot pot [L&C 14]

le/la pote friend, pal, buddy (mate) [4]

pousser to push (too far), to exaggerate [7, 10]

pousser: Faut pas pousser. Don't push your luck! [2]

prendre la tête to bore [L&C 7]

prendre son pied to have a lot of fun [7]

prendre un coup dans l'aile to have a shock [11]

prendre un pot to have a drink [L&C 14]

prendre un râteau to be dumped/dropped [L&C 7]

prendre une veste to be dropped, to fall flat on your face (to come a cropper) [5, L&C 7]

la pression draught beer [L&C 14]

Un prêté pour un rendu. tit for tat; One good turn deserves another. [4]

le/la pro professional [6]

que dalle nothing at all (sod all) [1, 6]

que tchi (keutchi) nothing (sod all) [6]

Quel bon vent t'amène? To what do I owe the pleasure of this visit? [4]

Quelque chose ne tourne pas rond. Something is not going quite right. [4]

la racaille rabble, riffraff, scumbag [6]

raccrocher to hang up (phone) [11]

radin tight, miserly [12]

raide dingue (de quelqu'un) crazy (about somebody) [7]

raketter to mug, to do over [6]

râler to complain, to whine, to moan, to nag [2, 4, 9]

le rap rap [L&C 9]

râper to fail [12]

rapido fast, quick [6, 8]

le rappeur rapper [L&C 9]

rappliquer to keep coming around [9]

le ras-le-bol the limit of what one can accept [2]

ras le bol: en avoir ras le bol to be sick and tired of something, to be fed up with, to have as much as you can take [2, 9]

râteau: prendre un râteau to be dropped, to be dumped (to get the push) [5]

le raveur raver [L&C 9]

recharger les batteries to recharge batteries [10]

régaler to treat someone else [14]

regarder: ne pas y regarder to be generous [14]

régler to settle up, to finish up [6]

remettre to have another [14]

remettre ça start all over again [2]

remonter (le moral) to lift your spirits [5]
remuer to stir, to get someone moving [2]
le rencard date, meeting [1]
le réseau network, Internet [L&C 9]
rester sur le cul* to be taken back, to be knocked over [9]
le resto (= restaurant) restaurant [14, L&C 14]
le resto de fête restaurant for a big occasion [L&C 14]
rétamé: être rétamé to be hammered, to be wasted (legless) [14]
retaper to cheer someone up (to give someone a lift) [5]
retourner sa veste to change your ideas [5]
le/la reub Arab (**verlan**) [5, L&C 5]
réussir un beau coup to succeed [8]
rien ne se produit nothing happens [4]
le rigolard joker [8]
rigoler to laugh, to joke [13]
les rillettes canned meat (made from pork or goose) [2]
rincer: se faire rincer to get soaked [2]
ringard corny, old-fashioned [11]
ripoux (= pourri) rotten (**verlan**) [5, L&C 5]
RMI (= Revenu minimum d'insertion) unemployment pay [L&C 9]
le/la Rmiste someone drawing the RMI [L&C 9]
le rond penny, dime (sou) [4]
le routard traveler, tramp [9, L&C 9]

s'arracher to leave [10]
s'éclater to hit it off together [7, 9], to get a real kick out of something, to have a ball [11, 12]
s'égarer to lose one's way [11]
s'empiffrer to stuff your face [8]
s'en jeter un to have a drink [L&C 14]
s'engueuler to shout at each other [13]
s'envoyer to throw back/sink (down) a drink [6]
s'envoyer (une fille/un mec) to get (a girl/a guy) into bed [L&C 7]
s'envoyer en l'air to make love [6, L&C 7]
s'envoyer un verre to have a drink [L&C 14]
s'investir to devote oneself to, to get wrapped up in (work) [10]
salarié in a job, wage earning [1]
le salaud bastard [2]
le saligaud* bastard [2]
le salopard* bastard [2]

Salut! Hi! [1]
SAMU (= Service d'Assistance Médicale d'Urgence) ambulance service [4]
la sandwicherie sandwich bar [L&C 14]
saturer to have had enough of something [2]
sauter une fille/un mec to lay a girl/guy [7]
sauver sa carcasse to save your skin [9]
SBAB (= super bonne à baiser) particularly attractive girl [L&C 9]
le scotch whisky [L&C 14]
scotcher to stick [12]
SDF (= sans domicile fixe) homeless person [L&C 9, 13]
se barrer to leave, to go out [10]
se casser* to split, to beat it, to leave (syn. **on se tire**) [2, 4, 9, 10]
se casser la gueule* to fall flat on your face (to come a cropper) [6]
se concocter to concoct, to hatch (a plan) [8]
se creuser les méninges to rack your brains [14]
se débiner to leave [10]
se décarcasser to bust one's back (a gut), to make every possible effort [9]
se défoncer to get wasted [14]
se faire (une bouffe) to prepare a meal [1]
se faire (une fille/un mec) to get (a girl/a guy) into bed [L&C 7]
se faire lâcher to be dropped, to be dumped (to get the push) [5]
se fendre la gueule* to split your sides laughing [6]
se fendre la pêche to fall down (about) laughing [6]
se ficher du monde not to give a damn about something [2]
se figurer: Figures-toi! Get this! [11]
se foutre du monde to make fun of someone (to take the mickey) [2, 12]
se fringuer to get dressed up [6]
se geler: se les geler* cold enough to freeze your balls off [2]
se grouiller to get a move on [14]
se le mettre au cul* to stick it up your ass (arse) [9]
se magner to get a move on [14]
se marrer to laugh [5, 6]
se mettre en quatre to bend over backwards [9]
se mettre en train to go (get) with the flow [14]
se payer to treat oneself [14]
se payer la tronche to jerk around, to make fun of someone [5]
se payer un coup to go for a drink [8]
se payer une bonne grippe to get a bad dose of the flu [1]
se payer une cuite to get plastered [1]
se payer une sale tronche to look really rough [1]

se prendre (un apéro) to have a drink [14]
se prendre la tête to get worked up about things [9]
se ramener to arrive unexpectedly [1], to get together [8]
se rétamer la gueule to fall flat on your face (to come a cropper) [6]
se rouler des pelles to kiss [L&C 7]
se rouler un patin to kiss [L&C 7]
se saper to dress smartly [11]
se sauver to leave in a hurry, to beat it [1, 10]
se taper to treat oneself [10, 14]
se taper (une fille/un mec) to get (a girl/a guy) into bed [L&C 7]
se taper (une sale tronche) to look dreadful [1]
se tirer to leave [10]
se tordre de rire to fall about laughing, to split one's sides [6]
sec: à sec cleaned out (without a bean) [4]
secouer to shake up [6]
secouer: n'avoir rien à secouer to take no notice [2]
shooté high (on drugs) [10]
shooter to shoot (drugs) [L&C 5]
le siège seat [4]
le sigle acronym [L&C 9]
le site web website [L&C 9]
smaké high (on drugs) [10]
SMIC (= Salaire minimum de croissance) minimum wage [L&C 9]
smicard someone drawing the SMIC [L&C 9]
sniffer to sniff [L&C 5]
la soirée rave rave [L&C 9]
solide: C'est du solide. It's something solid, durable. [7]
le soûlard heavy drinker, drunkard [14, L&C 14]
sourdingue deaf [5]
speedé stressed out [10]
le squat squat [L&C 9]
le steak-frites steak and fries (chips) [L&C 14]
stocker to save [L&C 9]
stressé (à mort) (totally) stressed out [6, 10]
suer to sweat [6]
super great, first-rate, terrific [4]
surfer le net to surf the Net [L&C 9]
le survêt(ement de sport) tracksuit [9, L&C 9]
sympa (= sympathique) nice, cool, super (mega) [1, 3, 13]

T'embête pas. Don't get worked up about it. [3]
T'en fais pas. Don't worry about it (don't go on about it). Don't let it bother you. [5]
T'inquiète. (= Ne t'inquiète pas.) Don't worry. [3]
les tablettes de chocolat "abs," six-pack [7]
une tache spot, blot, idiot, jerk (git, berk) [1, 12]
la tajine tajine [L&C 14]
tape-à-l'oeil tacky [8]
taper: Il me tape sur les nerfs. He gets on my nerves. [8]
tassé (bien) a good measure [14]
taxer to borrow, to bum (to scrounge) [4]
la tchatche chatter, talk, language [5, L&C 5]
tchatcher to chatter [11]
Te prends plus la tête. Don't worry yourself (your head) anymore about it. [8]
le techno techno [L&C 9]
tenir le coup to last [10]
tenter le coup to try your luck [8]
la teuf (= fête) party (**verlan**) [5, L&C 5]
la thune money, cash [4]
tienne: À la tienne. Cheers! [14]
les tifs hair [11]
la tire car, automobile [10]
tirer la gueule* to pout, to make (pull) a face [7]
tirer une tronche to pout, to make (pull) a face [13]
tomber à pic to come at just the right moment [4]
tomber sur quelqu'un to bump into someone [1]
top-délire fantastic, the tops [10]
tourner au vinaigre to turn sour [11]
tourner autour du pot to fish for something [4]
tourner rond to go well, to be successful [5]
train: se mettre en train to get in the flow [14]
traite: boire d'une traite (to drink) in one swallow [14]
trempé (jusqu'aux os) soaked (to the bone/skin) [2]
trimbaler to lug around, to cart around [10]
trinquer to clink glasses, to propose a toast to someone [14]
la tronche face [1, 13]
trop: être de trop to be a third wheel (to play gooseberry) [1]
le troquet café, joint [3]
trouver une combine to find a way around a problem [5]
le truc something or other [12]

Tu délires! You've got to be joking! You can't be serious! [6]
Tu m'aurais vu! You should have seen me! [11]
Tu parles! So what! [4]
tutoyer to say **tu** to somebody [1]
le tuyau piece of advice [1]
le type guy (bloke) [3]

un peu gros over-the-top [13]
une union libre cohabitation (extramarital) [L&C 7]

La vache! That sucks! (What a pig!) [12]
vache rotten luck [12]
vanner to wear out, to exhaust [9]
vaut la visite worth a visit [L&C 14]
vaut le voyage worth a journey [L&C 14]
vaut un détour worth a detour [L&C 14]
le verlan backward language [L&C 5]
le viande-grill steak bar [L&C 14]
les viennoiseries pastries [14, L&C 14]
vieux: mon vieux my old pal (my old mate) [1]
la virée trip [10]
virer to fire (give the sack) [8]
vite fait quick meal [L&C 14]
voler dans les plumes to launch an attack [11]
vôtre: À la vôtre! Cheers! [14]
vouvoyer to say **vous** to somebody [1]
le voyou villain, criminal (rogue) [9, L&C 9]

le web Internet [L&C 9]

Y a de l'abus. That's a bit stupid (thick)! That's going a bit far. [2]
Y a de quoi. Something is wrong. Something is the matter. [4]
Y a pas photo! It's obvious! You're absolutely right! [10]
y aller fort to go over the top [5]
Y a pas l'feu! No rush! Calm down! [2]

zéro: à zéro rock bottom [4]
zéro: Ça me fout le moral à zéro. That makes me feel really bad. [4]
le zinc bar [L&C 14]
le zonard dropout, (seasonal) traveler [9, L&C 9]

Select Bibliography

Duneton, Claude. *Guide du français familier.* Paris: Éditions du Seuil, 1998.

Girard, E., and B. Kernel. *Le vrai langage des jeunes expliqué aux parents.* Paris: Albin Michel, 1997.

Merle, Pierre. *Dico du français branché.* Paris: Éditions du Seuil, 1999.

Mermet, Gérard. *Francoscopie: Comment vivent les Français.* Paris: Larousse, 1999.

Richard, Pierre-Maurice. *Le français familier et argotique.* Lincolnwood, IL: NTC/Contemporary Publishing Group, 1997.